26

II

26 DAEMONS, REVISITED
CONNECTING THE STATIC PRACTICE TO
THE PROCESS OF EVOCATION

II

26 DÆMONS REVISITED
CONNECTING THE STATIC PRACTICE
TO THE PROCESS OF EVOCATION

THE
SORCERESS CAGLIASTRO
Blood Sorceress, Necromancer in the hands of 9

THIS BOOK IS
DEDICATED
TO STUDENTS OF
THE
SCIENCE OF
SORCERY

AND....

TO PITCHER JOHN
WHO HAS,
SO WILLINGLY,
CROSSED THE
LINE....

TO THE READERS....

This 'Revisit" of 26 Daemons serves the desires of the readers.... I have been asked to expand upon these 26 Daemons in the areas of technique and personal experience. In this revision I have done exactly that. I have also provided a clear connection between the evoking of Daemons and the use of the main focus of the work of the Blood Sorcery Bible VOL II, Striking the Target, the Practitioner and the **Static Practice.**

The first version of 26 Daemons was a simple list, a menu of 26 Daemons with whom I had worked and a basic statement of their talents, desires and how to evoke them. I did not expect that book to become hugely popular as I wrote it as a booklet, a simple list for my students to use. I performed no divination nor Sorcery on it – as I never do on my books. It took on a life of its own and became a very popular book.

However...

From feedback, it became clear that the information in the original version was not enough. It is my intention that this 'revisit' will fill the requests of readers for a more solid piece on the work of evoking and utilizing these 26 Daemons. It is my intention to have provided just that.....find it herein......

S/9

INTRODUCTION

This is a new world of study in a way, unsettling to the lettered, and otherwise conservative followers of the rules....

To study Sorcery at this level is to dedicate one's life to honing techniques and getting ready for a new normal, one filled with the potential of manifestation. There is not one among us that does not wish to throw our hands in the air and produce that which we desire. To say that is not the truth is self-denial....

Sorcery is power. If we did not want this power, we would not seek it out.

The most decadent form of Sorcery is Blood Sorcery, and the decadence becomes apparent when, through pain and the release of suffering, it pertains to the evocation of Daemons. This book takes the Practitioner on that path with an introduction to the usage of the Static

Practice as it also pertains to these evocations.

This book is offered to those who are interested in a serious look into the work of evoking Daemons at the student level and upward. That being said, it is NOT SUGGESTED reading for posers and fakers...stop it. When you *pretend* to be a Practitioner of this work you are a taker, a pure fool and one who will of course, eventually stumble and come into an action with one of us who lives in full dedication. Perhaps with me, and 26 of my closest friends...

I offer this work to those who practice and study, sacrifice security and entertainment for ability, and sit endlessly, on the floor of a dark room, honing their abilities to communicate with Daemons.

For those Sorcerers and Sorceresses, I shed my Blood.......

My books addressing Sorcery and works such as this one on Daemons are instruction manuals and brief glimpses into my world, lab reports of a sort and should be considered thusly. These books are not novels, therefore, I write them in whichever font suites the piece and in large font size because the information is overwhelming and the readers of my work prefer low light environments. I leave spaces because this information is a new normal, and the reader's eyes need room to rest. There, mystery solved.

This book is written by an egomaniac. It must be. What sort of modern day Sorceress would offer a new list of Daemons, sigils and all, for public use? The common thought is that only great and powerful mysterious kings and Sorcerers long dead can be trusted with this task, as only those protected by Death dare make such an offer, so that they are not subject to questions regarding the materials. Well, I am protected by none of those luxuries.

The only protection offered to me is data, fact and truth. This revised edition further explores and reports my experience with these Daemons – and I am willing to report it. It is that simple. 'Simple' may not be punctuated with the delights of drama – however 'simple' = truth.

COMMON DEFINITIONS (for clarity regarding the use of the words, EVOKE and EVOCATION....)

evoke
bring or recall to the conscious mind, conjure up, summon, invoke, elicit, stimulate, awaken, arouse, call forth, bring to mind

invoke (a spirit or deity).

This author's definition and choice of the word that will lead us into contact with these Daemons-

Evocation – to recall an entity to the conscious mind

In the Blood Sorcery Bible Vol II, Striking the Target, the Practitioner and the The Static Practice, I state my Theory:

THE THEORY

All thoughts, ideas and desires, and the movement of such, are composed of bits of matter of one sort or another - whether or not we are of a technological capacity to define, see or measure them.

Thoughts, Ideas, Desires....all have weight – and weight is **perceived** when it pushes up against another object or being. For weight – think energy, for 'pushing against', think resistance. **All energy works best against resistance.**

THE THEORY AS IT APPLIES TO DAEMONS

The key here may be to consider that entities <u>OTHER THAN</u> human, mammalian, reptilian and other carbon based liquid supported forms have thoughts, ideas and desires.

Definitions and other important bits....

Liquid Supported – (authors term) Living organic or previously living organic beings, in this case human beings, in or previously in a living vessel (body). This definition is constructed in comparison with Daemons who show no evidence of liquid/Blood etc. having now or previously been involved in the formation of their physicality. A black dust, perhaps carbon in nature, is often seen after their presence has passed through an area.

The common thought among theoretical physicists is (as I have been told as I state clearly that I am not a formally trained physicist) that seventy percent of the universe is dark matter, and thirty percent is light matter. Science states (loosely) that we have a basic understanding (difficult to define 'basic understanding' but let's roll) of approximately four percent of that which makes up the light matter, and no basic understanding of that which makes up dark matter. **If that is the basic understanding of the universe, are we really in a position to state that only carbon based individuals supported by liquid matter are capable of thought, ideas and desires?**

To that point it has been my experience that Daemons are functioning entities, albeit functioning at a wide variance of capacities.

+What if Science could offer to us Daemons, provable through data?

+What if science was perceived to be **that which is discovered** – as opposed to only that which is discovered *by scientists?*

+What if we deconstruct the idea of that which is a scientist, and allow ourselves to be one?

Consider the idea that we, the human population, made a new decision that potential scientific discovery was available to each of us who seek it, and that which we discover should, for the purpose of presenting fact, be held up to the same standards of repetition required by the lettered among us. In this model the idea that the exploration of science and resulting discoveries belonging to **only** those who have undergone a *specific and narrow corridor of educational experiences* would become invalid. If discoveries found by others outside of the university trained circle were considered worthy of further study, then others, perhaps even a broad spectrum of individuals, may be inspired to use their minds for these endeavors without concern that their efforts would not be supported and the resulting outcomes would not be considered relevant.

What if a Sorceress, not a theoretical physicist, looked at her work through the scientific point of view and procedure and produced a list of Daemons based entirely on the data gathered by usage?

Here we go....

I have been accused by some of harboring a great ego, and yet by others cautioned against giving my power away by these writings. I have been called an evil Daemon and a compassionate humanitarian both within the same day. This is anecdotal proof that there are no cultural universals.

Truth and discovery are attained by traversing the long hallway of opinions and confrontations.

My mind refuses to accept that a person must be singularly any one of those things. Daemons, like humans and other entities, are multi-faceted, bringing together collected experiences. What if, rather than looking for the many ways in which a Daemon cannot be like us – we for a moment look at their power – observe it and see how we can be more focused in our energy. Then we can all partake in utilizing the power to causes fear amongst the religious paranoids.

What if rather than seeking to separate ourselves from Daemons through fear and paranoid warnings, that instead we looked straight into their energy and welcomed it into the reflection of the core of our own battery – our own energy – what then could we achieve?

To this point, imagine if you will a ball of highly polished silver, reflective like a mirror, and in that reflection you see yourself - broadened by the curve of the sphere, seeing your reflection in the company of Daemons. Whose reflection is distorted and whose is not...?

> **I am successful with Daemons because I understand that I am built in the same complex form, yet, it appears, of dissimilar matter.**

Let the egomaniacal sharing of information and technique commence.

DAEMONS?

We, just as Daemons, are all amalgams bringing a unique set of conditions to our form, and yet it has been shown to me, by them, that it is delusional to think we can co-experience time.

Daemons experience time by only one determiner - by progress.

Daemons have a desire to become tangible. That is what they have stated. Therefore they perceive only the **progress of that effort** as the passing of time. To them - No development = No time has passed. Time is irrelevant to them unless they have been successful in their quest to add weight and form, therefore progress and relevance are proven, i.e. tangibility. Imagine if we, the great makers of timepieces, allowed ourselves to see it that way....

To see progress in evocation – we must be present – in control – and yet not in the way...

I offered the first edition of 26 Daemons from a data block of ten years. The book itself was a pamphlet, a quick gathering of data meant to report to the reader that there was great opportunity afoot with these untapped entities. There were many more Daemons during that period of time, however these 26 presented a case for this discourse by appearing on a consistent basis when evocation was performed in the manners listed herein. Now that I have produced material supporting the study and practice of the Static Practice in the BSB2, it behooves me to present that material in addition herein in a shorter form as it applies specifically to Daemons. That is the point of this exercise, to combine that which is now available to study with the work that can be achieved through evoking these 26 Daemons.

What are ten years in the life of the work of Blood Sorcery, as it pertains to the evoking of Daemons? For me as it pertains to this book, ten years is a solid block of time representing that which has contributed to the evolution of these Daemons who have made themselves available, involving their energy into the work. This second edition offers an extension of that research, having applied techniques of the Chaos Void, and the Static Practice to these evocations. Here is what I chose to do: to be straight forward and report that which I observed, and what I did to replicate the experiences utilizing these additional techniques. Therein is the ever evolving Science of Sorcery.

Ten years. In that time governments rose and fell, extreme weather became the norm, The Blood Sorcery Bible Volume One has been the coveted tome of the self empowered and the Blood Sorcery Bible Volume Two – Striking the Target - has opened the eyes of so many to the more advanced techniques of the work. In that time and continuing forward I, The Sorceress Cagliastro, have continued to pursue, experiment and report. I continue to use Blood and magnets, evoke Daemons, and with them I perform acts of Sorcery. It is just that simple.

Ten years is the parameter of time in which

these 26 Daemons presented themselves often enough to me for data to be gathered, Sorcery experiments to occur, and for this writer to present them in this writing as a personal experience of fact. Thus – the block of an agreed upon ten years, inside of 2002 – 2012 was useful for the accruing of data, and this new edition written two years after the first publishing, just at the twelve year mark, provides the inclusion of the Chaos Void and the Static Practice.

I have no way to prove that ten years is perceived as the same block of time to Daemons as it is to humans. All I can say to that point is that over ten years, as understandable to me, these Daemons entered my life in service to the work of Blood Sorcery in my hands and are still present in my life and my work. **These additional two years have shown them as they are now, responding to further applications of the Static Practice.** The Daemons themselves are the same. The evocations have become even further honed.

These 26 are current working Daemons. The sigils contained herein, are photographs of large format works which I have painted, tempting, perhaps even enhancing them with the desire to join me in Blood Sorcery.

WHERE ARE THE DAEMONS WE HAVE KNOWN FOR CENTURIES?

It has been told to me, and shown to me that all Daemons have a desire to manifest in some way, utilize or obtain a human form in which to explore and enjoy contact as humans do. They have expressed to me that they evolve, picking up more and more chaos and suffering which keeps them in motion. This motion reacts in a way to the magnetic properties of the earth and therefor they increase their ability to pick up energy. As they develop their energy they have a pseudo-tornado effect (poetic license), gathering matter in their path. It is from the point at which they begin this energy gain that ultimately leads them on their path to manifestation.

As time is only relevant to Daemons as it is expressed in **progress**, then there is no way for us to gauge the specific amount of time (as we see time) in which this transition may occur. My Attending Demons are old. "9" is ancient, as he explains, he is "older than collective memory", which I interpret to be older than the written historical record. In this time he has evolved into a higher level thinking Daemon. Most Daemons are lower level thinkers, by which I mean that they think only of that which will serve them and not that which will serve another. It is for this reason, this distinction of high and low level thinkers, and individuals such as 9 being a high level thinker, which separates the potential Attending Daemons type from the exclusively self-serving types. Daemons who have evolved into the higher level of thinkers are prepared to assist others full time without evocation, those are the ones who become Attending Daemons.

So what of the Daemons of, for example, the Goetia? Where are they now? I am often asked about the evocation of these Daemons. I find that most of the people who come to me seeking these Daemons are individuals who have tried and tried to contact them with little to no success. There are several theories....

One theory is they are no longer available for this work as they have evolved and are tangible, carnate, amongst the living.

A second theory is that they are now particular about from whom they desire their energy. They are evolving and able to pick and choose as they like. At this level of choice they can shape their eventual self-manifestation and the energy chosen along the way is important to that manifestation.

Many living humans have contacted me and made statements such as "I have summoned Paimon and..." or, "I have raised Lucifer..." and I say – really, you have? Tell me about it. They proceed upon some tangent about how they brought these great and powerful, masterful Daemons into their presence, and either enjoyed a sexual encounter or began an agreement regarding selling their 'souls'. At this point I ask them to define 'soul'. The answer is inevitably something about essence, sense of self, the part of them most like god and all of this sort of vagary. I ask them how they can sell something they cannot describe? How can they decide its worth? How does one know if one got a good and fair deal?

The flipside of that moment is when I tell them that IF they had summoned such a powerful force there would be an outcome, a tangible change somewhere between profound exchange of knowledge and bursting into flames. Neither, as you may have guessed, occurred in these individuals. I go a step further and ask them - if they had evoked such Daemons, in what way could they possibly need my assistance? Blinking....Blinking.....crickets....

Deciding that the only Daemons worth an evocation are the ancients is akin to the fabulous stories of reincarnation one in this work, often hears. Everyone who has 'reincarnated' (for the record I do not accept reincarnation as the Disincarnate tell me it does not happen) was Napoleon or Cleopatra – no one ever says they were the accountant, horse groomer or water boy.... Greatness is a powerful magnet to which many are attracted in the presence of that polarity. **Greatness however is built and climbed to – it is not mimicked.**

The point is that there are Daemons everywhere, and one should make use of the needy ones, the ones desperate for contact – as they will function in a manner set to please. Their motivation is delightfully selfish as they know that the more they do for the one who calls upon them, the more energy they will gather and therefore the closer they become to being tangible.

HOW THEY BECOME TANGIBLE

Daemons are tornadoes. Some are small some are huge and some are just first trying to pull themselves upright. At any stage they seek service and reek chaos and suffering so that they can increase their version of 'speed' (heightened energy). In this state of heightened energy they pick up more and more matter, and get closer to materialization, tangibility.

One way that this is possible is to do the work of the living human who evokes them. Daemons are best served by doing the work others will not do. Revenge, justice, any type of reconnaissance work, these are the tasks that pleasure them. Consider them also for the work of protection, especially if you live a life that inspires others, alive or otherwise, to seek to do you harm. Working against the resistance of this sort of on-going threat is very pleasurable to Daemons, most specifically to Attending Daemons. Seeing them at their best in this resistance offers a moment of thought regarding their interaction with physical energy and electricity.

PRESENCE

Daemons are less effected by light than the Disincarnate. The Disincarnate, for reasons we are currently exploring, become less visible the greater the light source. Currently we are exploring two theories regarding this matter, and those theories are for another publication. That being said, Daemons are not effected by light in this way.

If one removes the variable of the human eye processing them and interpreting the visual experience as Daemonic in form and nature, all that is left is a pure question of how light effects them on the atomic or subatomic level **apart from** our ability to perceive them.

Allowing for a baseline that states that Daemons exist, and that they can be seen, there is little data to suggest that they are seen in greater or lesser quantities as the variable of the presence of a light source is increased or decreased. In other words – Daemons can be seen anywhere at any time.

ON THE SUBJECT OF ATTENDING DAEMONS

Attending Daemons attach to living human beings very early in life, so most of us who are to have them already do even if they have not yet made themselves known to us. The work at hand is to open the portal between yourself and your Attending Daemon/s. I have had them since birth, and was of the privilege to have always seen them. For this reason I search for ways to assist others in seeing them, yet I have no personal experience regarding the launching of that ability.

My family situation was, at best, peopled by individuals with extraordinary rage and a lack of control of said rage. My Attending Daemons stood between me and that rage with such vigilance that I did not know that everyone else did not see them. I carefully crafted that sentence as I DID know that one family member saw them and spoke to them. One individual in my family was, as she put it, "set upon by the gifts" and unafraid. As time went on it became more and more apparent that to rage upon me was a bad idea, and the icing on the cake is few could figure out exactly what was the cause of their pain and suffering if they did act in a hostile manner toward me.

To live as a **protected child** is a unique experience. One develops quite soon into the fantasy of living outside of the law, away from rules, uncluttered by expectations of conduct. Then one takes on that life and it is no longer a fantasy. One grows into one's full self. That was my experience of decades of dedicated hard work and how I came to live this privilege.

WHAT HAPPENS TO YOUR ATTENDING DAEMONS WHEN YOU DIE?

Attending Daemons are unable to ascertain a finite line between the living and the Disincarnate. This is an advantage to the Disincarnate and a disadvantage to the Daemon. The Disincarnate enjoy a bond with the Daemon in free vision, without the clutter of the living human mind, with their Attending Daemons. They are freed from the vessel of the living and thereby they are able to explore a deeper relationship with their Attending Daemons. However, it has been made obvious to me that the Attending Daemon does not always have a solid grasp on the fact that Death has occurred upon the human to whom they attend. It is outside of their nature to understand Death as something of a particular transitory nature. To Daemons, Death is an event from which to, in certain situations, shop for suffering. The human who has Died or is in the process of Death does not interest them as much as the suffering does. It is as if they disregard the human all together and take in the energy of the chaos, suffering or other uncomfortable energies.

Post mortem, the Attending Daemon most often stays in attendance and does not gain momentum or tangibility as they are less likely to now be operating against resistance. They are not participating amongst living humans, not tasking and serving for them, so they do not evolve. As the Disincarnate become 'more of who they were in life once they are dead', the Attending Daemons remain attached, and on occasion continues to seek suffering. For this it will need to visit the living.

In a unique alignment of energies, this Daemon may be serving a Disincarnate who is of a mind to control the living. This is a powerful team. I will write more about this reciprocal relationship in another publication.

THE DAEMONS

Daemons, like humans fall into categories. There are those I pass in the street, unnoticed, un-recallable going about their day as I go about mine. We may see one another in the periphery, yet we remain uninvolved.

Another group is those who are part of casual encounters. We interact within the same pleasant distance as I would with someone from whom I would purchase coffee and good quality beef. A relevant yet brief moment, much like the face you cannot place out of their work environment, they are memorable in their function but not form. A nod of the head suffices and the beat goes on.

Next, a group of the reoccurring project beings, here for a while and then on to that which is next without the connection made by understanding their cravings. We share only the story of work what was perchance shared and nothing more. The relationship is swiftly built and swiftly dismissed, retaining a method of contact only if need be, brief work projects, coming and going.

Another group is filled with the nasty ones, the Spatters - those who are in it for the skirmish. They are endlessly entertaining if they are knocking at someone else's door. They are Blood thirsty as they know that the presence of Blood equates to the presence of suffering. They cause pain, confusion, miscarriage, loss and conflict from spats to full scale wars. They are to be avoided and only the most seasoned amongst us should participate in their energy. They will kill if killing suites them. They will maim just for a quick taste of suffering.

All of the Daemons who fall into these categories were not chosen to be mentioned in this book. They are too young or too chaotic for the purpose of work taught through this medium. Drawing on such Daemons may be a way to destroy your enemies, however without hands on instruction of how to block them from inhabiting you, there is no guarantee they won't demand more from you than you are willing to give.

Lastly there are Attending Daemons. They are pivotal in my work, and without them, most especially 9, I would endure injury, overwhelm and perhaps Death. As you have by now noticed, this second edition includes some language on the relationship between living humans and Attending Daemons.

The Daemons chosen for this book have appeared, stayed, worked, left and most importantly – made themselves available again whenever evoked, and during that time showed so much about themselves that rituals could be built for accurate repeating of these evocations. They are in a separate category I refer to as Reliables. Amongst them you may notice that I encounter and communicate with more male than female Daemons. There is no analysis or resolution to be offered on that statement. That data mirrors my life, as I am more prone to male friends and associates, and generally more involved in communication with masculine energies. This is a simple fact.

This book will also not address the Daemons commonly known or those published in ancient grimoires. Enough, in my opinion, has been written about them, and I rarely involve myself with them as, in all due respect, they seem best served by others of another discipline.

I don't know if they are still intact, as they have been utilized by so many humans. To be clear I am of the opinion that the reason many of them do not materialize is that they have fulfilled their desire, and have become tangible, perhaps human. However that theory itself is another book, another discussion.

NOTE...take a moment...consider this...

Here is your opportunity to be alone with twenty six Daemons about whom no one has written prior to the first edition of this book, and as far as I know offered their services to few if any other Practitioners until the publication of the first edition of this book. Through the publishing of that first edition others have had the opportunity to evoke and explore. These Daemons will have, due to that opportunity, grown in substance. I desire for this revisited writing to continue to serve them well so that they may encounter additional Practitioners and be heard or they will forever remain anxious for contact.

> **There is extraordinary opportunity here if the reader considers how these Daemon's urgent need for contact may result in their excited participation.**

WHO POSSESSES WHO?

There is a wide acceptance that humans are vulnerable enough to be possessed, or inhabited by Daemons. To be clear, an inhabitation is best defined as a portal the Daemon has created or accessed used to enter and leave the body of a human or animal at will, occasioning to do so when it is convenient. A possession is exactly what the word implies. One is in possession when one no longer has a will to override the Daemon's will for use of one's own body.

> What if the opposite were possible? If all thoughts, ideas and intentions have weight, then there is no substantive reason to accept that humans cannot put their cognitive self into the inhabitation or possession of a Daemon.

Daemons can be extraordinarily powerful unguided (not necessarily misguided) energies. Through ritual one can use a living thought and place it inside of one of these Daemons, these energies, and send it to task. This is not the same as making deals and asking a Daemon to task for you.

This manner of human possession upon a Daemon can, and has been done. To do so one is best served by evoking what can only be described as Daemonic **energy**. Perform an evocation to bring the **energy that powers** Daemons to you. To do so you must be in a state of physical suffering, be still and willing to enter into that suffering – as opposed to fighting against it. Stand on the line between the pain and the experience of the pain – the Chaos Void – and work the energy into the Static Practice. Pain is a curious experience as it is meant to show us that something is not as it should be. Pain signifies danger, injury, a directive to get help or flee etc. To have pain and stand inside of it is to take this power, harness it and control it.

SADEO MASOCHISM AND THE UTILIZATION OF PAIN

Sexual submissives who have a true connection to pain as pleasure are half way there. They can experience pain and redirect it into pleasure and ultimately into orgasm. To do so releases the energy formed by pain.

I performed an experiment with a full time lifestyle S&M couple. We decided to do six sessions where the submissive was put through various experiences by the dominant partner during which time I performed evocations. I asked them to use clear language so that the submissive would be in a state of control, only allowed to achieve orgasm post evocation. Going further through their process affords the submissive an opportunity to step into the pain, allowing the individual to stay with it and at this point set aside the sexual aspect and focus purely in the pain. In that manner of process, eventually the pain becomes chaos – i.e. uncontrolled energy. The submissive was asked to stay in it – not to turn away despite the aversion the human form has to pain. I watched carefully as the submissive turned the pain from torture to anticipation, pushing into it, feeling it press up against a desire for satisfaction. At that moment the energy was pure, the resistance (desire for orgasm) was clear, and the evocation was greatly enhanced by the process. Even during the evocation of random Daemons and/or Daemonic energy utilizing pain and sexual energy, as the energy works best against resistance, Daemons are attracted.

When you are face to face with pain, allow it to be perceived by your body as a presence, a heat perhaps. Pain is an important part of any discussion about Daemons, as pain, for most living humans, equals suffering, and Daemons are wildly attracted to suffering. Use this powerful energy in your work with Daemons. That is a method to the Static Practice.

PAIN...

When used in the evocation of Daemons, stay in, confronting it, and it becomes a physical sort of white noise which leads to chaos. Allow your mind to put the chaos in a void. Now you have it, now it is yours to use. When you are in this place, you are in the Static Practice.

Call deeply from your mind upon that which I will refer to only as **A Daemonic Energy Single And Vulnerable**. Take the first letters of each of the words of that phrase. The resulting trigger word is ADESAV. Use this new word as a trigger in this practice. Stay in, do not fall to the temptation of dropping out of this nothingness. You will see entities. They are the newly formed, the 'young' Daemons that arise every day from one crisis or twisted experience or another. **Lock your mind on one. Get inside of it. You are possessing a Daemon.** Task it from within it, tell it what you need it to do. Tell it how it will gain strength from this process, invite it to return for further instruction, then give it permission to go.

Breathe....

THE PUNCHING PIG – ANOTHER IN-SERVICE DEAMON

On September 19th, 2008, a Daemon showed up to communicate with me. This particular Daemon was in possession of the ability to physically touch humans, and lacked the intellectual ability to think and discern through more than very basic thoughts and processes. His appearance was that of a large bipedal pig. He often appeared in a cloth robe tied at the waste. There have been many tales of pig shaped Daemons in Christian theology, Japanese Daemon stories and so many others, that the appearance of a Daemon pig did not seem surprising to me at all. He became neither an Attending Daemon nor one that should have been on the list of 26 Daemons chosen for this book as he seemed to function best not when evoked, but rather through his own listening, observing and self-imposed vigilance.

The Daemon pig expressed one desire to me, and throughout our interaction I felt as if he had several humans with whom he had made an agreement to serve for a period of time. He wanted to enter the dreams of those who had crossed a line with me or anyone close to me, and give the offender nightmares which consisted of coming home and being met by this huge bipedal pig, and then experiencing being punched to near death by him. To me, this seemed like a workable and satisfying arrangement. Since his arrival he has offered this service and has done so via his own observation of those with whom I have interacted. His manner of work is thus that he will appear when I am experiencing a difficulty of interaction, ask if he may be of assistance, and then once I nod in permission, he will go about performing the nightmare. It is a comfortable arrangement.

One evening I asked the Daemon pig, who I began to refer to as Punching Pig, if there is a way for me to place myself in the room during the nightmare so that the individual receiving the nightmare would be certain it was from me. The Pig did not have an answer, however one of my attending Daemons did. TWO offered a ritual where I utilized hairs pulled violently from my head so that the roots would be attached. I was to burn the end of each hair at the end far from the root. The roots were then to be placed into my mouth while I slept, and it was made clear to me that if they fell out, if I pretended to sleep (why would I?), or if I did not follow through on the final part of the ritual that I may very well feel the pain of the punches the next time I slept. I tied them together with thread, taped the long ends of the hair to my face so I would not swallow them. I then taped my lips closed as not to have them drop out of my mouth. That night I had the extraordinary experience of entering a dream of another living human being while ACCOMPANIED by a Daemon, in this case the Punching Pig. The experience was similar to walking amongst the Disincarnate yet with a sense of being carried.

The final part was that I was to, upon waking, place the hairs on my bare thigh, cut into the flesh of my left arm and as the Blood from my arm dripped it had to pass through the flame of a wooden match, put out the flame, and the Blood must land on the roots. This had to happen three times. I did so and I will say that for reasons that must have been attached to the ritual, those three cuts were more painful than most cuts are. This was the harvesting not of Blood – but of Pain – the fee - as Daemons do not respond to Blood the way the disincarnate do having never been human. They seek suffering for their payment – and they got it. Those three cuts took longer to heal than any others, and have left a light permanent scar.

I was then to put the hairs and the scraped off Blood into a bottle of red wine and keep it outside for twenty days, after which I was to break the bottle on the ground letting the liquid seep into the soil. When I did so, the small bundle of hair was not in the bottle...

Try this ritual if you desire to enter dreams.... I found that it works with, or without the pig....

THAT WHICH YOU NEED TO KNOW

These 26 Daemons are unique as they have not been written about before, apart from the first edition of this work. Being new, in so much as they are new to the public, allows the practitioner some leeway and freedom to experiment with them without the burden of a thousand pages touting the claims of others. The evocations herein are also devoid of the need to memorize hundreds of pages of ritual text. These Daemons are more modern in the sense that many have offered information which allows me to decipher that some may have been formed in the twentieth century, and a few perhaps in the very beginning of the twenty-first century. Working with Daemons who are early, but not newly formed is like working with pure energy with just enough sensibility to allow for the making of extraordinary deals. Their eagerness is not the 'pick me' urging of the neophyte, nor are they well fed and tired. They are present and looking for their seat in the theatre....

These are not the Daemons of the Goetia, the GV, the Rouge or the Pullet. Many are younger Daemons, newer to their lot, so some may tend toward erratic behavior. This is however an opportunity to work with Daemons who may be eager to participate. Take heed and be prepared as some are not the most experienced of servants and others are in full possession of their anger, force or storm like manner. Now that this caution has been delivered I will say that if you were one to desire a predictable outcome in all that you do – you would not be reading a book on the evocation of Daemons. We are all adults here...... giddy up....

BLOOD SORCERY – One

cannot expect to read work written by me without encountering Blood Sorcery. We are all humans connected by this fluid, the Sacred Elixir, Blood. Through the use of it, Sorcery and evocations are more powerful and effective as the harvesting triggers that which is necessary in the mind of the Practitioner.

Blood Sorcery requires that you puncture your skin, or the skin of another in some way and use the Blood in ritual. For a more complete understanding of the methods of harvesting your Blood, read the book, Blood Sorcery Bible Volume I, Rituals in Necromancy. It is published by Original Falcon Press so you can find it there. All other techniques, specifically the use of the Chaos Void and the Static Practice can be found in greater detail in the **Blood Sorcery Bible Vol II, Striking the Target, the Practitioner and the Static Practice,** and is the one which is **more applicable** to the work in this book. End of commercial.

ACTUALITY SORCERY

If, as my theory states, all thought, actions, desires and intention have a physical weight, then creating a diorama of the situation sparks a fire in our minds. Physically building a scenario is another way to lean into the power of physics. If we perceive a particular life for ourselves with the full force of our will, Sorcery and an understanding of how physics works with us – then we will have exactly that which we desire to have. Include in your diorama the Daemons whom you need to evoke in order to launch the work and whose presence is an absolute requirement to create and fulfill a desired outcome.

To create a diorama of a sort is to be in the process of constructing a physical representation to be set to action by Blood Sorcery. There was a good, albeit fictionalized version of this in Beetlejuice. Do not wince away and chuckle about such a reference. We live in modern times. **Great Sorcerers take that which is around them and use it to their advantage.** If I referenced an ancient city whose cornerstones were still set into the ground and asked you to imagine yourself using it as a diorama by making a replica and placing yourself and your intended Daemons in the ruin, your intellect would be satisfied, however your outcome may have been unsatisfied by your distance from the materials.

Mentioning the diorama in Beetlejuice brought many of you to a place of complete clarity, a recognition of the description of the task, and most importantly, an understanding of the accessibility of this technique. This work is meant to be used in the daily lives of those who desire to call themselves Sorcerers. At this moment in time our daily lives are in modern times, and therefore modern references are valuable.

Some of my students have tried the diorama technique using virtual methods such as computer games and programs that provide an ability to create and people a living environment. Others have built elaborate cities, used children's doll houses, shoe boxes, one used toothpicks and straw dolls on a drawn blueprint.

The medium is irrelevant, the method is solid.

> **As the method pertains to Daemons -** Create the diorama to represent the **outcome,** and **move the players into place** representing a moment just before outcome begins. Walk the players through the outcome with suffering in place and you will accomplish that which you desire.

For evocations that represent long term or vitally important outcomes, make a diorama and have it present when evoking or possessing a Daemon as they are more visual than has been the common thought on the matter. Many have shown me they see that which is presented to them and they are able to evaluate it. Most of them are not of high intellect, so visual items can be helpful.

When showing them what you desire, be clear to speak the words, see the activity in your mind and show them who is who with your diorama. Harvest your Blood and place it in areas that represent you. You may desire to continue this activity using an entire table top of effigies and self-effigies in and out of dioramas in order to have an on-going experience with these Daemons. This technique is especially useful where space and privacy are at issue.... Offer them this Actuality.

A FEW MORE DEFINITIONS

DEMEANOR (more powerful than 'mood')

Daemons respond to suffering and visuals that seduce them into thinking they are about to encounter more suffering. I mention it here as that simple explanation gives the reader an additional visual tool when thinking about how to connect the Daemon to the desired task through a selective manner of evocation.

Think for a moment about seduction as an

illustration of demeanor. Then consider seduction in motion. One may consider the erotic movements of a belly dancer, circling the tent, hips swaying, body undulating, arms inviting the observers to come closer. This sort of activity is meant to raise the erotic temperature of a room. It is clear. It is not meant to urge the audience to think of their mortgages or illnesses, commitments or disappointments, it is movement focused upon intention.

> **When evoking Daemons, choose the demeanor most perfectly aligned to the desired outcome, and you will attract that manner of Daemon willing to do that work.**

INHABITATION – the
experience of a Daemon or other entity utilizing the human vessel as it pleases without causing a presence which completely overtakes the human being. There has been an established portal so the

Daemon can enter and leave at will. An individual experiencing inhabitation finds themselves with new or unexplainable desires and habits, black outs, memory loss, and often comes back to a conscious moment without knowledge of that which has transpired. The human being can have a communication with the entity that has inhabited it.

POSSESSION – the experience of the complete takeover of a living human being by an entity. In possession a human being is not in control of their thoughts or actions. The entity takes over and suppresses the personality of the human being causing it to appear as if the human being is no longer involved in the use of their own body.

SORCERY EVENTS – Rituals and processes gathered together to create a specific act of Sorcery

DARK & LIGHT SORCERY

Ahhh the great myth... All Sorcery is dark as all Sorcery is manipulation. There is no good or bad Sorcery, there is only one's interpretation of the Sorcery at hand. If you are enacting Sorcery and the Sorcery you perform will change the path of another either directly or through a series of related outcomes, even healing, then it is dark. Accept it and have a drink...

DISINCARNATE – the dead

DAEMONS – Demons may be a more familiar spelling. They are an amalgam of energies wrought from suffering, confusion, chaos, angst and other discomforts.

KARMA – Don't waste my time with this nonsense. If we are to be powerful humans set this ridiculous notion aside and take responsibility for your own actions

right here and now in real time. A weak mind accepts that all acts will balance out, punishment will fit the crime – through the righteousness of a floating genie set upon the situation to sort it all out later.

Practitioner - you

26
Daemons

These are Daemons with whom I have developed relationships, ongoing, private, and now, some public, trusted or negotiated, easy going or strategically dangerous, all relationships none the less. For each of the 26 Daemons herein, I offer data on each of them in the following areas:

SIGIL –developed to represent the Daemon. If the drawing of the sigil is required in ritual those directives are included. If not, draw the Sigil in the book in which you document your work. If you are struggling and cannot successfully evoke a particular Daemon, harvest your Blood and paint the sigil on a material that is in alignment to the likes and proclivities of said Daemon.

HISTORY/STORY – Some of the Daemons allow a glimpse into that which has created them. I have included that information wherever possible. The ones who do not offer this information may or may not know their own back story. Some of these Daemons know, and are not willing to tell their story. I respect that. Humans should consider offering less back story.

HOW TO IDENTIFY – visual description of the Daemon.

ELEMENTS/MATERIALS OF PREFERENCE

Those elements or items that have proven to aid in the summoning of that particular Daemon. This information has been gathered through any manner of input, trial and successes and the like. In some instances the elements are part of the environment, supporting the space so that the Daemon will feel a general comfort when entering. Others are specific to the ritual. Remember to keep as many of those elements and recommended items as possible in the space working as they act as additional bait.

Also keep data on any additional materials which may have supported the effort and use when repeating the ritual.

DESIRES – the type or category of activity the Daemon would prefer to do on their own or on behalf of the Practitioner

DEFENSIVE ACTIONS REQUEST
– evocation used to call upon a Daemon to enact justice or some such act upon another living human.

TRIBUTES – gifts or actions Daemons require from the practitioner in order to perform the work

DEALS – Daemons enjoy making contracts or deals to bind the practitioner to the commitment by negotiation. This may be done for fulfillment or for amusement, and noted where applicable.

EVOCATION METHOD - based on repeated successful evocations.

AN INTERACTION – My personal experience with the Daemon and/or additional information. This is what the readers asked me to provide.

NOTE – the following Table of Contents lists Daemon's area of effectiveness. The

work can be directed at yourself in a productive way or at another in either a constructive or destructive fashion.

The names of the Daemons have been presented to me by the Daemon repeatedly over time. I DO NOT chose their names. When the name is a number or a combination of numbers and letters, those numbers and/or letters have been consistently presented to me by the Daemon and in those cases no other identifying moniker has been offered.

Table of Daemons

1 MERCURICAX
effects human primal behaviors

2 G'HERY
controls breathing, regrets and guilt, focusing abilities

3 HOLLOX
manipulates genetic traits and technology

4 147H
alters appearance, weight and machine-like strength

5 AYST
thief Daemon, deal maker, thug

6 BURNT
drains away color physically and theoretically with brutal calm

7 TEVID ALTIER
perfection and redistribution of extraordinary wealth

8 GOLOX
strengthens or weakens bones, balance, and ability to compete

9 KERM
manipulation of visual images and maps

10 FERVERE
manipulation of the written word, legal documents and evidence handling

11 EXTREME HEAT
increases speed, sexual passion, investment activities. This Daemon uses forward moving momentum only.
CAUTION ADVISED

12 442
alters muscle strength and mass

13 SKIN 67

physical protection from known and unknown attackers and detractors, sexual development

14 SUGAR

the baiter, manipulates conception and Corporeal Necromancy (CAUTION)

15 NOHG

the soldier, the assassin

16 AXE 22

Silence, stillness, deafness and Death

17 908ST

sexual prowess, shape-shifting

18 JACK 558

Canine elements, friendship and leadership, wolf connections

19 843
provider of sustenance (no reverse attribute)

20 HIHH
double or extreme peripheral vision, increased Sorcery abilities

21 SCREW 779
manipulator of gravity and aging

22 PITCHER JOHN
dangerous boy, sharpens or distorts memories or one's ability to remember, controls bees, wasps and hornets
CAUTION –
HE LEAVES ONLY WHEN HE IS READY TO GO

23 FLYD GLUTD
controls freedom, escape or fleeing, use to get paroled or to imprison

24 188

remove or cause stress and tension on individual or group

25 Serp-Hant Ave'

A delicious Daemon of epicureanism, intentional selfishness, self-appreciation or vanity

26 CHAGATATHY

controls armies, war strategies and egos, controls the minds of soldiers and followers

ONE
MERCURICAX -
effects human primal behaviors

HISTORY/STORY - He states that he is the combined remnants of a group of slaughtered families from a military takeover of a small town in the Fourth century, Europe. From the sound of his voice and an indescribable innuendo I feel he may be speaking of having come from France. His description produces the feeling and the mental imagery that perhaps a hundred people were slaughtered, living in family units of ten or so. He states that the town specialized in the making of metal tools although his language is not modern. He, in our very first interaction, caressed and pet the iron tools on my altar and moaned when doing so. He meanders about the room in a state of deep and profound sadness and comes as close to crying as I have seen a Daemon able to do. His moans are low, deep however not soft or passive.

Mercuricax describes that he "grew" from the seed of the last living human lifting his head and seeing all the dead, most specifically his sons, slaughtered around him. From that moment the human he speaks of didn't pass to the world of the Disincarnate through the proper channels. On his path to doing so he spun in rage and gathered the fear and hatred of the slaughter with great force creating the Daemon Mercuricax. He says his name is a combination of some of the names of the town's elder men but about this he is not sure as it was moaned and bellowed by the dying in desperation. More recently he has said that the dying were angry in a profound way while stating this word.

HOW TO IDENTIFY – Mercuricax appears as a small muscular bull with a human head, and an ability to stand upright. His body twists suddenly and spontaneously without any warning subtle or otherwise. He has a scent like wet soil which has been pounded and lived upon by animals.

ELEMENTS/MATERIALS OF PREFERENCE – Iron, vinegar, human and feline Blood on thick grass

DESIRES – He encourages us to strengthen the most primal behaviors within ourselves including protection and awareness of impending danger. He is sexually overt and will perform acts of Sorcery that encourage or require a sexual component. Do not fall prey to his sexual presentation. To do so will give him power over you.

DEFENSIVE ACTIONS - Mercuricax can be called upon **to strengthen the Practitioner or weaken core strengths in adversaries** in the following areas: sexual prowess and virility, ability to perform Sorcery, fertility, physical strength, stamina

TRIBUTES – Mercuricax requires that you give feed to a starving animal. That of course is open to your interpretation.

DEALS – If you do his bidding and provide Tribute, he will perform a Desire or Defensive action for you or on another on your behalf. His deals have never been on going in my experience. One deal for one action completes the transaction.

EVOCATION – Note - Mercuricax does not particularly like human beings. Keep interactions as brief as possible. When working on yourself, bait him with any of his elements except vinegar, and use only vinegar when working to weaken another. He is enticed by a slow hand drumming on an animal skin drum. As you drum develop a beat that is comfortable for you to use when saying his name over and over. He will be very clear if you quiet your mind and listen. You may smell him before hearing or seeing him. Be aware of his movements. Do not let him make physical contact with you as he is powerful and not very graceful. I would go as far as to say he spasmodic. To create space between you and he push his elements away **with force** to let him know you do not seek physical contact. He responds well to this sort of rejection. He is very sexual in nature so be cautious of these overtures unless you seek such an interaction. Know that if you become sexually involved with him he will desire to continue and then he will be in control.

When you are SURE he is in the room tell him of your desires. This Daemon in particular does not respond to your desire unless he is fully present. Continue drumming consistently and make no sudden movements. When he is the room he can be easily agitated so do not evoke him unless you are in a quiet place with no interruptions. Tell him what you desire. Tell him multiple times until he is still. When he is still he is concentrating and hearing you. Tell him when you are done. Slow down the drumming to a gradual stop. When you do not hear, smell or see him any longer he has accepted and is gone. If he leaves while you are talking he has not taken the deal. Mercuricax is very solitary in nature and will go when the deal is made.

AN INTERACTION

Evoking Mercuricax can be a cathartic experience because of his sexual nature. After an interaction with Mercuricax I find that I have a heightened sense of smell and an even clearer ability to see one's true intent.

At first I thought that Mercuricax left an emotional hangover of sorts and perhaps even a sense of paranoia. The fact is that the experience is quite contrary to that first analysis. A heightened sense of that which surrounds one is a gift he leaves, intentional or otherwise as he is not particularly verbose regarding this matter.

He also leaves a sense of a heighted sensuality, not so focused on the desire for sexual contact but rather in the sense of sensuality inside of oneself surfacing and having a presence. So to that point it is an option to utilize the evocation of Mercuricax in a more casual manner, offering him an opportunity to visit without instruction. Making your sensual presence known to him serves his need for contact as well.

TWO
G'HERY – controls
breathing regrets and guilt, focusing abilities

HISTORY/STORY - the most I can gather from the little G'Hery has said of his origin is that it is related to a connection of the final exhale (last breath) of humans and animals and that the heavy sighs, tears, sadness of all sorts have been, and continue to be gathered into feeding this Daemon's energy.

HOW TO IDENTIFY – G'Hery is a mist at first, followed by a sigh and the outline of a cachectic human. Lately he has begun to make a huffing sound between words as if he is displaying his breath.

ELEMENTS/MATERIALS OF PREFERENCE –
smoke from incense, ash from burnt newsprint, humid and sea air, oyster and clam shells, white flight feathers from large birds, preferably tropical and/or white birds

DESIRES – G'Hery desires to keep the practitioner in the moment, in good respiratory health, and confident about one's work moving forward. **He can be quite useful in sharpening focus where distraction occurs.** Although it is not in his spoken repertoire, I get a sense that he can be of some assistance with the desire to increase Sorcery skills and Divination.

DEFENSIVE ACTIONS – Evoke him to cause others to struggle with breathing, feel faint, lose focus on their work or mission (good for war strategies big and small), cause dizziness, worry and feel regretful to the point of an interruption of daily life. If a human is on their final stage preceding Death, G'Hery can be called upon to allow them a swift completion of the activity known as Death.

TRIBUTES – Burn lightly scented non floral incense during his summoning and for several days after the work is done.

DEALS – You must have oyster shells filled with sea salt present before evoking. A night must then pass prior to evocation.

EVOCATION –Make a dark earthy incense including cones or galls and burn it on coals within an oyster shell. Breathe in the incense until you find it is making you cough or feel discomfort in breathing. Keep the ashes, you will need them in this evocation. Turn away from the incense and using a pin, make a small puncture above your left breast. Lay flat on your back on the floor, smear the Blood with a finger from your right hand, offer your right hand up and ask him by name to "appear to me G'Hery (ga-herry) at my insistence and at this offering". You will feel suddenly cold starting with an icy sensation in your hands. Your head may suddenly pound and then you will become dizzy. The cold will travel through your body and then dissipate. Tell him your desires. Be clear, and if you feel inspired to whisper, do so as he often prefers a whisper to full voice.

Simply wait, breathe, and do so until you feel you are alone, breathing easily, no longer dizzy or cold.

When you are in that experience then you are done with him. Smear ash over the wound and walk away with your back to the oyster shell. Do not look at it again until the shell has gone cold, then bury it along with the coal remnants and he will be off to do the work you requested. You must complete this task. If not he will linger and effect breathing in an unpredictable way for anyone in your home including your pets.

AN INTERACTION

G'Hery and I work best together when dealing with controlling the breathing of another for purposes from healing through punishment and revenge. For these purposes I have called upon him many many times. Every interaction with him effects my breath and stamina in one way or another, some of which feel too personal to report.

Evocation has also proved fruitful in the area of increased abilities regarding Sorcery and a general ability to learn. I have been experimenting with G'Hery regarding opening up one's ability to learn a language. So far the results are data showing an increase in retained information in language studies. I find this works best with a language that utilizes an alphabet other than the one used in one's native language.

THREE
HOLLOX – manipulates
or alters genetic traits and technology

HISTORY/STORY – Hollox tells a story about coming into being as the result of the pain, fear and suffering of laboratory and service animals, but his story changes frequently including stories of slaughter and animal sacrifice. The contradictions in his stories are detail based, and block the user from understanding how old this Daemon may be. Animal suffering is the consistent thread. I feel that the inclusion of laboratory animals in his story is just that, an inclusion, and that his origin precedes the use of animals in laboratory/experimental ways.
.

HOW TO IDENTIFY – One hears a clicking noise followed by the scent of musk, and occasionally glimpses the thin semi-transparent outline of what appears to be a baboon.

ELEMENTS/MATERIALS OF PREFERENCE –willow wood, paper, semen, hair

DESIRES – alters or activates genetic traits and disrupts the performance of technology devices

DEFENSIVE ACTIONS – Hollox is a master of manipulation causing a lack of focus or implementing confusion. He can also control the suppression or activation of hereditary disorders. Hollox is also helpful when trying to conceive in the face of genetic disorders.

TRIBUTES – Blood Sorcery is absolutely necessary.

DEALS – makes none, unpredictable duration, suggest that which you desire - If more is asked for by Hollox, it has to be an immediate transaction with nothing lingering as Hollox will manipulate you through it if he has something over you.

EVOCATION METHOD – Harvest Blood from your scalp and use it to paint

Hollox's sigil on leather or some kind of skin that is not dyed. When it is dry wear it against your flesh for at least 24 hours. You may find that you are nauseous during this time. Next, in a quiet place and making sure you are alone, hold the sigil to your lips, Blood side facing you, and speak your desire. It you see him it will be done. This is a simple transaction. If he appears repeat the request and tell him he can go. Keep the sigil for future communication with him. If he does not appear he does not want any part of your request. In that case, bury the sigil deep in the earth and wait at very least several days before trying again.

AN INTERACTION

Born with a hereditary disorder of the neurological type which I have conquered completely with Blood Sorcery, Hollox was instrumental in maintaining that complete release. Hollox came to me during the process of removal of the genetic material which supported this anomaly.

FOUR

147H – alters appearance, weight and creates machine-like strength in humans

HISTORY/STORY – 147H states that it developed from vanity, the pain and torture of "147 million mirror images". 147H is genderless and without form. It is a Daemon comprised entirely of energy with tremendous power which may be disproportionate to its age. 147H appears to be young as there is no solid formation. However that could be an effect by choice based on the fact that the formation came from vanity. This Daemon states that the destructive force was not the use of the mirrors but the obsessive use and the sense of disappointment.

HOW TO IDENTIFY – When successfully evoking you will see the number/letter combination 147H as a three dimensional form. If 147H is reaching out to you, the number 147 will appear often in a short period of time.

ELEMENTS/MATERIALS OF PREFERENCE – glass, mirror, highly polished silver metals

DESIRES – none that have been made apparent other than a willingness and desire to be commanded in the area of weight, appearance and strength

DEFENSIVE ACTIONS – 147H can weaken the opponent significantly in the long run. It can be a relentless Daemon.

TRIBUTES – A new mirror must be kept in the space until the work is done, after which the placement must be of a personal nature, such as a bedroom or sacred space.

DEALS – work with 147H requires no additional deals

EVOCATION –To summon do not eat and become as hungry as you can handle. Place yourself in a cold or otherwise uncomfortable place and say the following: "Every bite, every morsel I taste brings me closer to 147H"

Then have a small bite of a favorite food. Feel yourself craving more, and when you cannot tolerate the craving any longer eat another morsel. Do this until 147H appears. The harder you push, the greater the sacrifice between bites, the better the outcome. If 147H does not appear then wait at least 24 hours before you try again. Like most Daemons, 147H will not appear unless you are sincere and likes the request you are proposing. When 147H is there you will hear a verbal response that is deep and rumbling and will feel as if it is churning within you. The response will be brief so listen carefully. Respond with your desire. Wait. If you do not hear a response then your desire was not of sufficient interest to this Daemon. If you do hear a response then respond in kind until the agreement is made. When the discussion is over eat handfuls of food in a vulgar manner. This will cause 147H to want to leave.

AN INTERACTION

147H is very useful in strengthening and shaping the human form. Right at the time of this writing I have just begun to utilize this Daemon in the reshaping and strengthening of my own form. Going forward I would like to utilize 147H in the area of physical therapy for a control group who has suffered injuries requiring rehabilitation.

After summoning 147H I I feel a sense of increased height. The experience is entirely cerebral as the data of my measurements shows no change. However the value to the experience of a sense of increased height comes with increased strength and a connection to warrior energy.

FIVE

AYST –thief, deal-maker, thug

CAUTION

HISTORY/STORY - Ayst is a very dark, tricky and angry Daemon, and the Practitioner should take care to make very exacting deals in this situation - and stick by them. Ayst rose from the practice of cutting off the hands of thieves. This is a very unpleasant gathering of energy. Ayst has been in formation since the second century. He is short tempered and able to work only in small bits of time. Be very specific. This is all business, do not try to make friends. He can turn on you and there is a significant risk of inhabitation or possession.

HOW TO IDENTIFY - Ayst appears as a little boy, formally dressed, and the era of his clothing changes not only from evocation to evocation, occasionally it will change during the session. He is sullen and his mouth does not move when he talks. He keeps his head slightly held down and raises his eyes when his thoughts are to be heard. His arms never leave his sides. His movements are wooden in nature, stiff as if he were a toy brought to animation by a ritual gone wrong.

ELEMENTS/MATERIALS OF PREFERENCE – wood, liver and coal

DESIRES – Ayst doesn't care about your integrity or any proof of action. If you say someone stole from you then he will work to justify the matter. That can work against you if you lie as it appears he may have an overseeing Daemon that reacts to his work if it is unjust. This is not a morality warning as I do not indulge in them. This is a warning regarding your well-being. Ayst will do exactly what you ask for if he is interested, and that is without boundaries. His overseeing Daemon is seen occasionally, not always, and is unpredictable as well. The experience gives one the sense that he has an Attending Daemon. I have never seen that before or since.

DEFENSIVE ACTIONS – Ayst punishes those who have stolen from you and his work delivers obvious painful and damaging results

TRIBUTES – Ayst, oddly enough, requires that you steal something. Choose carefully and go as benign as possible.

DEALS – He will do your bidding if you do not bother him with the emotional drama of how you feel about the theft. Keep to the facts.

EVOCATION - Stand on a wood block outside or in a room without technology or electric appliance noise, and no clocks of any kind including your cell phone. Place a piece of coal in your pocket. Stay very still with your arms at your side, head down, eyes to the floor and say this or something like this rhyme which juxtaposes what happened to someone who had his hands cut off for a petty crime.

Here is to the man who took my hands
Little boy sad where he stands
Left a family with untilled lands
I take vengeance where I can

When he appears using coal "write out" your desire on the palm of either hand in big overlapping letters. Be specific. He can correct the situation and/or punish the doer. If you do not know the doer, this is the time to ask him to reveal the name. **He is one of the few on this list with Divination abilities.** You will hear the name if he knows it. If your hand begins to feel warm or burns he is willing to participate. Listen carefully and he will tell you that which you need to know and that which he will do. He will instruct you from where to harvest Blood and when he does, do it and wipe it on the coal. If he does not want to participate then he will fade away. Bury the coal either way or he will stay and that is neither a good or safe situation. When you hear that the work has been done through whichever channels you receive information, speak of it with no one so you will never be thought to be attached to it.

AN INTERACTION

Ayst really is a deal maker and a thug, and therefore knows best how to assist other deal makers and thugs. If you have clients who are in touchy legal situations, especially those who are under observation regarding, perhaps, family ties to other individuals who have been known to be involved with crime families or organized crime, then by all means consider an association with Ayst. He understands the nature of these connections and has an extraordinary sense of strategy and technique regarding potential solutions to these matters.

On the flipside, he is very motivated for justice. Consider working with Ayst if something has been stolen from you. Appeal to him expressing your loss regarding a theft. Make it clear to him that the loss represents more to you than the simple loss of the item. Ayst responds to the sentiment of loss as it pertains to theft.

If you utilize his skills in this way be prepared to witness justice. Leave your moral compass at home and keep your sunglasses on as slipping away from being noticed in this interaction will best serve both of you. Ayst enjoys covert justice and revenge.

SIX

BURNT – drains away
color physically and theoretically
with brutal calm

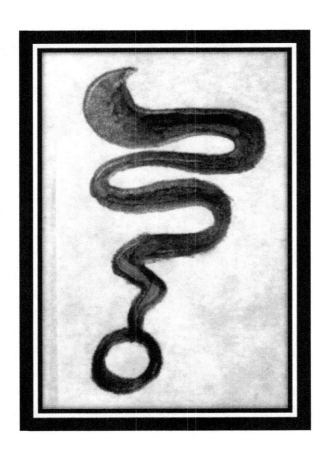

HISTORY/STORY – Built from the energy of Death by arson. This is a female beetle with a male energy.

HOW TO IDENTIFY – a large black beetle with one silver or shiny eye and one black eye

ELEMENTS/MATERIALS OF PREFERENCE –
Alcohol, sand, bitter herbs, human bones

DESIRES – Burnt desires to answer evocations from those who can work without regret. This is of the utmost importance. If that is not genuinely who you are stop now and choose another Daemon.

DEFENSIVE ACTIONS – Burnt can burn down a structure, or sap all the energy from a person or project. She can do so quickly or slowly over an exhausting period of time.

TRIBUTES – apples left at the base of trees in wooded areas, empty envelopes

DEALS – You must tell someone you did this work with her and not be dissuaded by their reaction.

EVOCATION – To properly summon Burnt one should keep a beetle or at very least a Madagascar Hissing Cockroach, Walking stick, or some form or exotic beetle or bug. Obtain this creature and treat it well if you feel that Burnt is a Daemon with whom you will have a long term working relationship. Burnt is one of the few on this list that is welcoming of long term interactions. Do not use a spider, scorpion or worm. Burnt does not care for them. Take very good care of the insect you choose. If you cannot keep such a creature you must at very least find one and collect leaves over which it has walked.

If you do keep such a creature, place into its enclosure several loose leaves that can dry out. If you cannot keep such a creature, then collect leaves over which a beetle has walked. Grind the leaves and combine them with wood incense base and rough salt crystals. Set the mixture on a rock and burn until it goes out. Take the remaining dust and draw Burnt's sigil on the outside of an empty envelope and while doing so, say aloud that which you desire. Leave the envelope upright and opened in a place in which it will be undisturbed. Wait until 24 dry hours (no active rain or snow) and check the envelope. If Burnt will do your bidding, there will be a bit of dust or ash inside of the envelope. The work will happen and Burnt will not linger. If he has agreed you must tell someone of these events and from where you received these instructions.

If you desire a long term relationship with Burnt, then keep the incense and burn it on occasion without asking him for service.

AN INTERACTION

If you are having an experience with someone who will not go away – a stalker – an individual who drains you and is aware of your desire for a disconnection yet will not honor that desire, then Burnt is your Daemon of choice.

Burnt was evoked in the case of the client who had been raped by a neighbor and walked away from legal punishment due to a technicality in his arrest even though he admitted his guilt. Burnt took care of the justice portion of this interaction.

Also consider evoking Burnt to transfer the energy of someone to yourself. This is a manner of punishment or justice that is very effective. Use it wisely, saving if for situations which serve you best savored in slow motion. I find that after using Burnt I feel satisfied, relaxed and accomplished in a pure and sincere way.

SEVEN
TEVID ALTIER -
Daemon of perfection and redistribution of extraordinary wealth

HISTORY/STORY – Tevid Altier developed from the human struggle surrounding the making of art and the deciphering of messages written in codes.
.

HOW TO IDENTIFY – Tevid Altier is a woman of goldfish yellow skin with deep yellow gold hair. She wears a white transparent dress made of what appears to be glass, however it moves with her. She is barefoot and her feet are cut in multiple places both on the top and bottom. She carries a short wand of sorts, or a stick (as I have never seen her use it in any way). It looks comprised of amber and wood.

ELEMENTS/MATERIALS OF PREFERENCE – broken glass and wood chips

DESIRES – for the practitioner to be able to complete a project, feel perfection for at least a moment, and obtain wealth from that moment

DEFENSIVE ACTIONS – Tevid Altier can cause another to lose focus from their work, and to experience pain in traveling (walking or standing). She can also make art supplies unattainable. Her most delightful ability is redistribution of wealth. If one has millions, and a Practitioner feels they deserve it, evoke her to redistribute it.

TRIBUTES – Prepare by using glass instead of plastic whenever possible. Plastic kills Sorcery as it is not particularly conductive. Tevid Altier requires the practitioner to be surrounded by glass. To be effective evoke near windows, glasses, glass objects of any kind OR while standing in a box of broken glass, (I won't bother with the caution here as it is obvious).

DEALS – You must finish your project, or follow through on this task or she will destroy your artistic abilities and redistribute your wealth. She is quick and can be mean.

EVOCATION (Read Tributes for location) Break a glass or bottle. Cut a small incision the back of your left thigh with the largest and sharpest remaining piece of glass. Cross your legs so that the Blood appears on the front side of your right leg. Smear the Blood to cover an area of your skin and once it is dry write her name in the Blood with a black pen or quill and ink. If you are using quill and ink, add a drop of your Blood to the ink for additional honing. If she appears she will do your bidding. If not, she feels your desire is beneath her efforts. Re-examine your desire and improve its depth before summoning her again.

To release her all you need to do is complete your end of the project.

AN INTERACTION

Once upon a time there was a girl working as a maid in a great big apartment in Manhattan's upper west side. After three years with the family the husband began to make sexual advances toward this young woman. The distribution of power was, clearly, not creating an even playing field.

After a year of avoiding his advances she succumbed as he had convinced her that her residency status and her economic situation lessened her safety so she gave into a sexual relationship with him. She conceived a son. He gave her a sad amount of money and told her to go away. Her fears took over and she took the deal.

Her mother contacted me from Eastern Europe. She told me the story and I met with her daughter. She explained to me that she could not afford a lawyer and was afraid of the man who fathered this child due to his enormous wealth. Tevid Altier was evoked. The wealth has been well re-distributed. It was a three Vodka martini celebration....

EIGHT
GOLOX -
strengthens/weakens bones, balance, ability to compete

HISTORY/STORY – The energy of Golox is derived from amputations and tomb raiding. There is an overtone of Egyptian influence in Golox.

HOW TO IDENTIFY – A tall staff appears, silver and blue, and in the right light one can occasionally see the holder which I have come to understand is manifested by the Practitioner so it is different entity for each of us. Caution the apparition is derived from ones greatest fear yet there is almost a sense of Anubis here. (As I wrote this a silver staff rolled across my table and vanished.)

ELEMENTS/MATERIALS OF PREFERENCE – silver, human bone.

DESIRES – Golox desires to remain detached from the Practitioner, no friendship will be formed here. Do not attempt to push this point or Golox will weaken your bones.

DEFENSIVE ACTIONS - To empower oneself, create or completely destroy another in a profound way. She is a Daemon of extremes. She is also useful when **WIN** is desired in a competition. She enjoys the sounds of bones rubbing together and breaking so be careful.

TRIBUTES - Agree to bury that which next dies deep in sand. Be careful as if that which next dies in your world is human that may be difficult to accomplish. (Pour sand into the casket if all else is not possible). Therefore think very carefully before summoning Golox. The tribute is a powerful requirement here. If it is not fully met she will take something from you – and she will determine what it will be.

DEALS - CAUTION - **The weight of that which is asked to created must be, at some point, balanced with a request to destroy and visa versa.** The problem with that is that we do not know when we will die, so making this agreement is tricky. I suggest one does not summon Golox until one has **both, one create and one destroy** desire at the ready and can ask for one following the other. Golox says if these directives are not followed due to the Death of the Practitioner she will cause great pain for a remaining living human with whom the practitioner is deeply connected. If the Practitioner is still living, she will enact this justice on the Practitioner at her whim.

EVOCATION - Being naked in complete privacy wearing only silver adornments, burn an incense of high tones, drink red wine and say something like:

Golox I cannot pretend
To care for those who wrong me
Do that which brings vendetta

Or

Golox create new life through birth
And make this new one tamable
Let its feet walk the earth

All of these phrases are only triggers meant to focus the Practitioner. Keep that in mind. We are not suggesting magical words or tonal sounds here.

She will show you a staff and it will move from a vertical position to a horizontal position if she will do your bidding. Keep all deals and she will leave when those deals are completed. Until then she will linger and watch you.

AN INTERACTION

Several years ago there was a foolish man who decided to cross my family and I in a manner that disrupted our home setting. I informed him that I would respond accordingly. He, being an attorney, felt he has the upper hand.

He enjoyed competitive bike races and boasting about his bully behavior. During his boasting he said that someone who did the "make believe crap I do" should be "grateful for whatever leftovers society throws my way" and that if I wanted to get into a fight about this I "wouldn't have a leg to stand on"....

I suggested to him that language is a wicked weapon and he did not take heed. He continued in his rant regarding the mocking of my chosen life's work. Every comment he made regarding my work was followed by a more vulgar comment debasing myself and my family as if we were lesser beings than he.

Well, Golox and I decided to start with gout. The gout became so pervasive that part of his right foot was amputated less than one year later..... Who still gets gout? And by the way – now who doesn't have a "leg to stand on?"

NINE
KERM –manipulation of
visual
images and maps

HISTORY/STORY –Kerm is actually twins, one male one female, human in form, created by the panic of finding oneself lost and revisiting the same dead end or lost trail. Kerm has expressed this formation through a visual demonstration. They are chaotic twins acting out a horrible story of being lost and dying in a forest.

HOW TO IDENTIFY – when Kerm is present the blood vessels beneath your skin become more pronounced.

ELEMENTS/MATERIALS OF PREFERENCE – wax, metal measuring devices, fine parchment, tobacco, brass or bronze coins

DESIRES –clarity in direction and finding appropriate lodgings

DEFENSIVE ACTIONS – Call upon Kerm to cause disorientation, utilize Actuality Sorcery, illustrate or create a diorama

TRIBUTES – the sigil must be written on parchment in your Blood with a device containing genuine brass or bronze.

DEALS – you will have to spill your Blood three more times, at intervals demanded by them

EVOCATION - Using pre-existing objects, or making your own from wax, wood or wire, create a diorama of the event depicting the desired outcome. Keep it in a safe and private place and **DO NOT MOVE** it once it is completed. When the three additional spillings of your Blood is complete so will be the Sorcery at hand. At this point the diorama must be buried top down in a wooded area. If it is not done just that way Kerm will cause disorientation in the Practitioner.

AN INTERACTION

KERM – my darling twins..... When I am on land that pours forth the Disincarnate or Daemons I call to Kerm to show me graves that are hidden by time and need acknowledgement.

Nights that I have spent in graveyards of all types have been enjoyed in the company of my twins...Kerm.... One distracts guards, making me invisible to them. The other stands upon the graves that need attention or the ones that harbor remains locked and confused – unable to understand communication. Together we open these portals. Kerm leaves me grateful, even more than I usually am, to be in service to the Disincarnate....

TEN
FERVERE -
manipulation of the written word,
legal documents and evidence
handling

HISTORY/STORY – Fervere is comprised of all the angst and persecution writers have experienced, and fueled by the writings of proclamations and religious decrees of damnation including misdirected prosecution through legal papers and improper evidence handling.

HOW TO IDENTIFY – Fevere appears as red discs that look like large wax seals.

ELEMENTS/MATERIALS OF PREFERENCE – ink, dark berries, sloe berries, gold rings worn by one owner for many years

DESIRES – To offer service that leads to the completion of written works, correction of legal documents, truth in evidence

TRIBUTES – the sigil must be written on parchment in your Blood with a device containing genuine gold.

DEALS - None

EVOCATION - Combine ink with a drop of either semen, Blood or menstrual Blood of a person who is a successful writer or artist. On the best quality parchment you can obtain, write exactly that which you desire. Sign it in the most elaborate way that fits you. Paint Fevere's sigil in the same ink on another piece of parchment and leave it somewhere in your home where it can be seen, and where you **do not** sleep. The document best serves the Sorcery when left in a book that predates the Practitioner's age. Leave in a library or vintage book shop book. Do not revisit it. If you have done this correctly your desire will be met by Fevere. If it is not met, try again using one of the other choices for biologicals.

AN INTERACTION

I have an agreement to keep interactions with Fevere completely private.

ELEVEN
EXTREME
HEAT

– increases speed, sexual passion, investment activities, CAUTION ONLY MOVING FORWARD

HISTORY/STORY – This Daemon has evolved from gathered sexual energy, slowly curated and utilized over many centuries.

HOW TO IDENTIFY – Extreme Heat appears behind the Practitioner's closed eyes as a slowly turning wheel with a fire burning in the center. It speeds up and slows down at will. He is neither kind nor forgiving and wants to rush everyone through their lives.

ELEMENTS/MATERIALS OF PREFERENCE
sulphur, ground smokey quartz crystal, shark skin, pure oil, gunpowder

DESIRES – to create fires and cause something to speed up, obtain sexual gratification, expertise etc.

DEFENSIVE ACTIONS – speeding up time can be useful if used sparingly and in very specific situations. This Daemon will allow you to do so but use sparingly. You can also take away another's ability to enjoy or perform sexually.

TRIBUTES –sacrificial burning, mammal materials

DEALS – For any time that is sped up, he will ask for you to live another time twice as slowly. Listen carefully and make a wise deal if you can. For Sorcery of a Sexual nature, he will ask you if he can enjoy some of your Blood. Remember to demand that he tells you exactly what he intends to do with that Blood and let him know you know he is really only interested in the suffering.

EVOCATION - The sigil must be scratched into your body somewhere below the waist, hidden, and must be allowed to become irritated or reddened. Use a sterile object for the scratching. Overheat yourself in some way, bring yourself to a frenzy through tears or dance or whatever works for you. Keep your eyes closed and use this phrase to demand the action.

Time is attached to heat
And burns with equal frequency

When you see the sigil behind your closed eyes, the deal will be offered. Stay quiet and still and agree only to that which you can handle. If you break the deal you will not be one hundred percent well ever again. You will always feel just 'under the weather'. Work carefully here. If the deal is satisfactory the Daemon will leave you alone and complete the task. Do not tend to the wound of the sigil for 24 hours.

AN INTERACTION

Clients frequently come to me regarding their libidos and other issues of a sexual nature. Evoking Extreme Heat has proved successful regarding these matters. I have begun adding the requirement to work facing east with this Daemon as the east facing polarity supports the speed of the work required by Extreme Heat.

TWELVE
442 – alters muscle strength and muscle mass

HISTORY/STORY – 442 reveals very little regarding a back story. All that has been revealed is that this Daemon is the result of injury to muscles and to discarded dead animals. It revealed nothing about its gender if there is one at all.

HOW TO IDENTIFY - the number 442 will appear either forward or backward in a red circle

ELEMENTS/MATERIALS OF PREFERENCE – Suffering garnered by the sacrificing of human Blood, pain through biting

DESIRES – to feed upon the Sorcery you perform and develop into a named Daemon. Everyone gets paid.

DEFENSIVE ACTIONS – can cause muscular strength or weakness, development or destruction

TRIBUTES – sigil written on wood in your Blood which has been harvested by puncture

DEALS – 442 demands physical exertion beyond any point of which you may have previously exerted yourself. Together define what that means.

EVOCATION - The evocation of this Daemon is performed over time. Draw this sigil with your Blood every single day asking for that which you desire. When you get it follow the deal agreement. **If you don't keep your agreement 442 may reverse the outcome of your desire to less than you had when you began.** 442 is an **unstable** Daemon in the process of gathering greater energy. It wants you to work through it, but be advised: although Daemons with unstable energies often provide the very best and most powerful outcomes, as they are proving their worth. There may also be some uncontrolled tangential energy. This book was nearly 25 Daemons as I thought very carefully about adding 442. While I was in the planning stage we had an interaction that convinced me 442 was reliable as it pertains to being able to be consistently evoked, however you can still sense the wild instability. You will learn Daemon control through work with these sorts of Daemons.

AN INTERACTION

I intend to incorporate 442 into the work I am doing with 147H. A sigil is under development to involve both Daemons in the restructuring of my body to my liking. Should I find that this process works as I feel it will, then I will publish the findings.

THIRTEEN
SKIN 67 physical
protection from known/unknown
attackers/detractors, sexual
development

HISTORY/STORY – SKIN67 is the result of medical fertility experiments in the nineteenth century. This Daemon is female in form.

HOW TO IDENTIFY – SKIN67 shows herself in the form of the appearance of a hand held shield accompanied by an overpowering scent of roses.

ELEMENTS/MATERIALS OF PREFERENCE –
Vodka, gin, rose water and Absinth combined

DESIRES – all forms of protection, development of one's own eroticism

DEFENSIVE ACTIONS – use to combat another's invasive vanity or actions, or to the detriment of one who constantly criticizes. This Daemon is effective against people who chip away at one over time and is able to distract potential attackers on the physical level. Use also for sexual development or manipulation.

TRIBUTES – In order to appease SKIN67 you will have to shave off a small piece of skin, put it in a vial, and cure it with vodka. It must be kept prominently on your workspace.

DEALS – She may ask for things such as desiring that you drink alcohol more frequently or shatter glass jars. Her demands seem random.

EVOCATION - Drink one of her materials of choice until you begin to feel the effects of the alcohol. Observe your face closely in a mirror. The mirror must be bigger than your head. Pour alcohol over the area of your skin you have shaved for the tribute. When the pain begins demand her services. She will speak to you directly. Be clear about your demands. If she is going to serve you the pain will stop. If she is not the pain will continue in a normal manner. If she does not serve you, consider another Daemon. If she does serve you she will do so over twelve – fifteen days.

AN INTERACTION

Wear SKIN67 like armor. I decided to use SKIN67 often in my protection work. Doing so has put this Daemon at my fingertips and no ritual is needed any longer to call her into place.

Fear is irrelevant. In the moment of that which we perceive as fear, all energy is available to be redirected through refocusing on a strategy to relieve the situation. Those strategies can be well thought out or spontaneous in a moment of necessity. These moments of necessity are when I call upon SKIN67 to drive directly into the situation and dismantle its power and energy. Develop a relationship with SKIN67.

FOURTEEN
SUGAR – the baiter, conception manipulator re: fertility and Corporeal Necromancy (CAUTIONS INCLUDED)

HISTORY/STORY - SUGAR is a Daemon from a life of slavery. She comes from the struggle of women who were abused in that situation. She deals with the unborn

HOW TO IDENTIFY - a simple female silhouette in a white dress. She always appears in a three quarters stance, never revealing her face full on.

ELEMENTS/MATERIALS OF PREFERENCE
white fabric, sterling silver, granite, tulips

DESIRES - to have control over conception (which has a broader meaning to include all that is newly developing)

DEFENSIVE ACTIONS - She can be evoked when one wants to control conception, or when one wants to bait someone into a pregnancy

TRIBUTES –Tend to graves of infants left in disrepair.

DEALS – If you ask to conceive you must be serious about taking forever care of the child. She will torture your life if you do not follow through.

EVOCATION - Whether you are male or female, you will need another woman to join you in this work. If the Sorcery is for fertility, ideally the woman who is participating should be the person who is trying to conceive. If you are the intended parent (mother or father), you will still need to do the ritual on the other woman and let the rhyme reflect that you are the person for whom the work is to be done.

First soak cotton fabric in menstrual Blood, let it dry and tear it into strips. The Practitioner must tie the strips together to make a knotted binding rope. It is best to have an odd number of pieces and should be at least three feet long. Remember all of these actions are triggers. Ask the woman who is assisting to lay on the floor in the fetal position. Her ankles must be bare. Leave a few inches hanging and use the binding tie to tie her ankles together in a figure eight motion, finishing by tying the final end to the piece left open in the beginning. Draw the sigil on both of her shins with your finger dipped in whole milk. Breast milk would be perfect for the task but very difficult to get. Breast milk creates a mental trigger that stimulates hormones. Thus the science of Sorcery....

She speaks in rhyme, so I wrote a little rhyme to summon her. You can of course write your own as Sorcery is about triggers that create a sufficient amount of thought energy to manifest desires. Chant your rhyme, (or this one) adding specifics if you like. This singsong rhyme shakes the Practitioner into a more relaxed state.

There is a child sleeping in the dark

Bring her forward bring her on
Maybe it's a boy maybe it's twins
Bring it forward everyone wins

Work yourself into an involved state of mind as you repeat your chant, and cut the ties with a sharp knife at the crossover point. Gather up all the pieces and use them to wipe the milk from her shins. **Bury the rags in the grave of a stillborn. That detail is very important as it involves the Disincarnate so it is more than a trigger.** Tell the individual who is to conceive to begin having sex or in-vitro (or whatever method they are using) once the rags are in the ground for two sunsets.

EXPERIENCED NECROMANCERS ONLY

CORPOREAL NECEOMANCY – include the name of the identity you desire to be reborn in the rhyme.

CORPOREAL NECROMANCY NOT USING BIRTH, do all the same, use VENAL BLOOD instead of menstrual Blood and bury on the grave of the individual you intend to raise. Harvesting Venal Blood requires a phlebotomist. Do not try to do this alone. There are many additional steps to this process. I offered this much here as I wanted to begin to show the reader the complexity of this work. To perform this act, communicate with me directly.

Further words of caution.
BE CAREFUL REGARDING THAT WHICH YOU WISH FOR.

THE ONE YOU RAISE WILL NOT BE CONTROLLABLE AND WILL NOT BE AS YOU REMEMBER THEM whether or not you use their body or put them in the recently deceased body of another.

When you perform Corporeal Necromancy you are responsible for the experience of the raised individual. PUTTING A RAISED DISINCARNATE BACK IN THE GRAVE IS NO SIMPLE TASK AND REQUIRES A SACRIFICE YOU MAY NOT BE WILLING TO MAKE.

AN INTERACTION

SUGAR is the Necromancer's Daemon. I turn to Sugar whenever I am in a difficult or sensitive situation regarding Daemons and the Disincarnate. I wear her sigil in a Blood talisman which I am not willing to describe.

SUGAR is unpredictable around living human babies. Therefore utilize her skills more often on the unborn or the empty womb seeking to carry an infant.

There is so much to say about SUGAR. A Necromancer should develop a profound relationship with her. She is one of the three on this list with whom I have opened a permanent portal of connection. This is not the same as an Attending Daemon as these three Daemons work exclusively in their comfort zone as Attending Daemons work to help and protect their living human.

If you work with SUGAR you begin to feel a melancholy about her, a connection and that connection is your finger touch on the Disincarnate.

FIFTEEN
NOHG – the soldier, the assassin

HISTORY/STORY – Nohg rose from the sorrow of Death on the battlefield and the tears of the parents whose mourn their children. The era of his origin is not clear but his mannerisms are not modern **THIS DAEMON CAN POSSESS YOU** as it is in his desire and his nature to do so.

HOW TO IDENTIFY– Nohg first shows up as a hot wind, stinking of rot. If he stays, and he rarely does, wait quietly until you can see a metallic outline of a man.

ELEMENTS/MATERIALS OF PREFERENCE –
Long pins, sharp knives, yew wood shavings

DESIRES – to let the dead know they are dead

DEFENSIVE ACTIONS – summon him for Death Sorcery, Insanity Sorcery, or Sorrow Inducing Sorcery.

TRIBUTES – caretaking of gravesites of soldiers

DEALS – You must tell someone of your work with him and they must keep the secret. It is tricky, you may have to make a side deal with the listener to make sure the deal is kept.

EVOCATION - This is a difficult evocation because it involves a lot of preparation and the pulling forward of a skill few have. Take into your hand a black metal (iron, steel) and concentrate on his name, saying it in a barely audible low grumble specifically emphasizing the OH sound in Nohg. You do not have to wait until you hear or see him. Once you feel steadied in the repeating of his name in this manner, roll the metal around in your hand and speak your desire. If he has heard you the metal will feel hot and may even bend or warp. When you feel this happening place the piece of metal on a surface made from any of his elements. Using a pin, harvest Blood from the top of your hand near the knuckles. This will hurt. He seeks the suffering. Drip one drop of Blood onto the metal. It may sizzle. If you do not do this part of the evocation you may allow for inhabitation or possession.

Complete the ritual and use the piece of metal to puncture something that is living such as a leaf or insect. This is Sorcery and it is not without its share of investments in the organic living world. Set the punctured item out in the elements to whither or be taken by prey animals.

AN INTERACTION

NOHG can kill. He may make that choice **after** you set him on to task.... Use if you can handle that outcome. If you cannot, choose another Daemon.

SIXTEEN
AXE 22 – Silence, stilling, deafness and Death

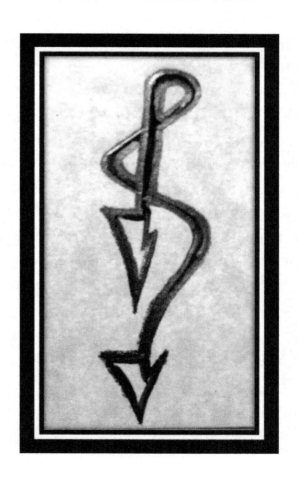

HISTORY/STORY

– This Daemon AXE22 came to me of his own will in a rage at the moment when I needed to see just such a creature. He offered his services to me when I needed to still a detractor whose actions were no longer acceptable. His rage was pure, blue-white like ice, sharp and undeniably brilliant.

HOW TO IDENTIFY

- He has the black gauze look of a Dementor from a Harry Potter film. If that reference seems silly, then you are not a Sorcerer who understands that inspiration and Sorcery input is just as possible from modern works as ancient ones. He moves with an agility yet is substantive as if he is a top heavy kite riding a very powerful wind.

ELEMENTS/MATERIALS OF PREFERENCE

– iron salt water and venal Blood

DESIRES – to do the bidding of the practitioner

DEFENSIVE ACTIONS – to do the bidding of the Practitioner (intentional repeat)

TRIBUTES – Venal Blood

DEALS – You must ask and act within the amount of time told to you by this Daemon. He is wild and brash and each interaction is a new beginning.

EVOCATION Consult a phlebotomist as you will need a vial of venal Blood. Get it, paint his sigil as this sigil is, more so than most, an impression of what he appears to be. It is in a way a portrait, a twisted energy with what appear to be hand wrought iron points at either end, almost as if he is a life sized garrote with some manner of a head in the center.

Using your Blood mixed with a bit of black ink (gall ink if possible) draw his sigil on something made of iron. Tie the item to the end of a rope or some kind of handmade or rustic length of cord, and swirl like a dervish saying his name repeatedly in a long low vibrational manner. As you spin you will encounter an area of the spin where the iron item slows down or seems to get snagged. That is Axe22 trying to snatch the venal Blood. When you are sure where he is, stop, face him and tell him you will trade the Blood for the task. Lay the item down. If he accepts it will move or become damp. Listen carefully. When you have heard demands and/or made agreements leave the item where it is so he may fondle it and scrape off some of the venal Blood. Then throw the item into a body of salt water. If you are not near an ocean, send it in a paper envelope to someone who is and tell them not to open it – just throw it in. If you do not complete this action then AXE22 will not leave you and you will begin to feel dizzy and weak....perhaps indefinitely....

AN INTERACTION

AXE22 can also kill, and is even more likely to want to than **NOHG**. He is a perpetrator in his own right. I have noticed an increase in strength in these two years in AXE22, more so than most on this list.

To use AXE22 note that he is likely to want to know the individuals with whom you discuss or perform Sorcery. He has a sense of impunity. He is not for the beginner to evoke as he is strong and focused.

Caution given.....as always it is up to you....

SEVENTEEN
908ST sexual prowess, shape-shifting

HISTORY/STORY – A Daemon of sexual energies, who I witnessed rising from a corpse of a slain sex worker at the Office of the Chief Medical Examiner. Her name reflects something that was found on the body. **This is a rare 21ˢᵗ century Daemon.**

HOW TO IDENTIFY – A varied group of birds or a woman in a feathered headdress with a high pitched laugh

Elements/Materials of Preference – feathers, Blood from the human torso gathered through pain, sea water, civet

DESIRES – to create a continuous sexual energy and allow for shape shifting or the illusion of shape shifting

DEFENSIVE ACTIONS – use to control another's sexual desires or to shape shift

TRIBUTES –give money to sex workers without receiving services

DEALS – None. This is a short and concise interaction

EVOCATION - best summoned during sexual activity. You need not tell a partner but when she appears your partner may see her and that will break the energy. Best if you call to her by tracing her number in your and you lovers combined sweat or body fluids. Combined saliva will also suffice. Tell her of your desires. When you see her the agreement is made. She will not stay. Keep up your end of the tribute. There is no discernable retribution if you do not keep up your end of the bargain. It is my suggestion that when working with Daemons, one always do so. This is a very young Daemon and we do not know what her evolution may bring.

AN INTERACTION

908ST is the absolute best path to shape-shifting. The use of feathers kept on my body is helpful when asking her to participate in shape-shifting as she is much more interested in sexual prowess. Feel free to use her abilities in either way – however be careful as she is very seductive.

If shape-shifting is what you desire be very clear about it. If not, and if you are open to it, she will take you on a journey. I am open to it because to be open allows me to have experiences with Daemons that teach me new skills or hone skills I already possess.

On several occasions working with 908ST I have found myself in a visual stimulation deeply kissing a woman. This woman is always the same so 908ST may have an ability to present to you that which you will find erotic. I have asked others who work her and only one other person has had this experience. The question is not fully answered as the person who also had this experience reports physically feeling the experience yet not seeing the woman. I am interested in discovering whether or not this is the same figure consistently. If this occurs when you are evoking her, you may continue to do so to enjoy this experience as that exchange of energy does provide 908ST with energy from which to grow.

During interactions with 908ST I have also discovered that Civet smells more tolerable, of a sweeter muskiness and not as pungent. This experience leads me to ask the question about how much she will alter the environment to seduce the Practitioner. Gather data on 908ST as she is very complex in nature and abilities.

EIGHTEEN
JACK 558 – Canine
elements, wolf connection, friendship and leadership

HISTORY/STORY – JACK558 is formed from sorrow accumulated from the Deaths of all dogs, wild and domestic. He is a young Daemon, not in years but in experience with humans, and is in on-going development. He told me that he has been wandering since 1493, and is bothered by this modern day development in which dogs are killed for lack of placement.

HOW TO IDENTIFY – He appears as a medium sized mixed breed with ears that tip at the top. His snout looks like a Irish Wolf hound but his body and legs are too short for the breed and his hindquarters slope downward.

ELEMENTS/MATERIALS OF PREFERENCE – bones, crushed beetles and river fish

DESIRES – to create a visceral bond between animals and humans

DEFENSIVE ACTIONS – to teach an animal how to protect you or how to turn raise your own ability to be unconditionally protective

TRIBUTES – He best serves you if you are in service to canines. This is not the Daemon for cat people. He seems to look at a person's life history with dogs and serves them thusly.

DEALS – JACK558 is best served by an overt act of generosity to a canine or group supporting canines, adoption, food, medical bills or support in some way is appreciated. Taking on A canine as your own would be the best deal.

EVOCATION - Obtain as many of his elements as possible and sit with your legs crossed and your head down in a quiet place. If you have dogs do not add them to this scenario. Live dogs do not mix well with this evocation.

Think of his name. In your mind offer him bones, crushed beetles and river fish and imagine his presence. He will appear calmly and quietly, at a distance at first. If he feels trust he will come closer and you will see movement in the elements you have left for him. Speak gently as you would to a feral animal. Do not make eye contact. Allow him to eat or sniff the elements if he desires. When trust is gained and he has agreed to help, you will feel him brush up against you. The more contact he makes with you the more he will do for you. When you are done, wait for him to leave the room, however if it goes well that could be a while as once he chose to sleep with his head on my thigh for several hours.

Once you contact him the first time, he will make it easier each time you call upon him. Give the remainder of his food to the forest or to an animal in need. Jack558 has a loyalty about him. He will leave at the end, however he may visit without evocation. At first I thought he may become an Attending Daemon, however he did not.

AN INTERACTION

I am deeply involved in working with JACK558. The canine energy is hugely important to me in my life and work. Currently he is still a working Daemon, however he has made overtures that have once again brought up the issue of his desire to be an Attending Daemon.

If you know of an animal abuser, and in this case more specifically canines, he will come down hard on them if you are clear about their identity. True to canine form he seeks a master so give him all the information you have and he will follow those commands.

As he is of huge service to canines as well as to those of us who are caretakers to canines, it is my sincere desire that he stay in the broad work of assisting all who call upon him.

NINETEEN
843 –provides pleasure, sustenance

HISTORY/STORY – this Daemon makes reference to points in history that have led me to think that this Daemon is no less than 3000 years old in formation. He rose from the "loss of food during a great and devastating flood" so his work as a deliverer of sustenance fits him, however his ability to bring pleasure seems anathema to his mannerisms.

.

HOW TO IDENTIFY - the appearance of his number in smoke or in some other slightly out of focus medium

DESIRES – to provide pleasure and sustenance

DEFENSIVE ACTIONS – to create sexual tension

TRIBUTES - none

DEALS – give food or pleasure to someone who is in need

EVOCATION - summon exactly as one would Daemon 17, 908ST, with male energy. The Evocation is repeated here for your convenience with gender corrections.
ADDITIONAL EVOCATION SPECIFICS
He is best evoked during sexual activity. You need not tell a partner but when he appears your partner may see him and that will break the energy. Best if you call to him by tracing his number in your and you lovers combined sweat or body fluids. Combined saliva will also suffice. Tell him of your desires.

When you see him the agreement is made. He will not stay. Keep up your end of the tribute. There is no discernable retribution if you do not keep up your end of the bargain. It is my suggestion that when working with Daemons, one always do so. This is a very young Daemon and we do not know what his evolution may bring.

AN INTERACTION

In this past year I have seen 908ST present while evoking 843. A stronger amalgam may be happening. Observe and be cautions as this amalgam would produce a very powerful Daemon.

TWENTY
HIHH – double or extreme peripheral vision, increased Sorcery abilities

HOW TO IDENTIFY –you will begin to experience dizziness and notice a metallic sent

ELEMENTS/MATERIALS OF PREFERENCE – steel, aluminum and leaded glass

DESIRES – fame, to be seen, and to raise the Practitioner's abilities. Hihh wants to be a visually present Daemon and seeks usage to increase his power and presence.

DEFENSIVE ACTIONS – to create confusion or distortion and to make another's Sorcery turn back upon them.

TRIBUTES – wearing and surrounding yourself with leaded glass objects especially when summoning him

DEALS – Hihh makes deals that are very private and individual

EVOCATION – make a small incision from the center part of your scalp. With the middle finger of either hand drag the Blood down through your forehead, down the center of your nose, through your lips and chin, and continue to the base of your neck, dividing your face in two with this dividing line. With the tip of your finger draw his sigil large scale (the sigil will be invisible as you will not actually be drawing it with the fluid) and lay face down in it. Turn your face from side to side in intervals of twenty or thirty counts, repeating his name and demanding his service. At one point you will feel a sudden urge to flip over on your back. When you do you will see some form of a ladder or web that appears to be made of chain. Inside of your mind, climb in. The rest is between you and HIHH including what he requires to leave.....

AN INTERACTION

HIHH is also useful to provide the Practitioner with a visual ability to zoom in like a zoom lens. This is accomplished by requesting the ability during the evocation. This ability doesn't last very long each time, however I have discovered that doing it often allows the Practitioner to call upon it when needed even if one is not in the action of evocation with **HIHH**.

The technique does not, at this writing, appear to have any side effects.

TWENTY ONE
SCREW 779 -
manipulation of gravity and aging

HISTORY/STORY – This Daemon is the result of the fear passengers experienced during an airplane crash in 2005. **She is a 21st Century Daemon.** She is the combined energy of fear and not knowing that one has died. She is still a bit confused and can be unpredictable.

HOW TO IDENTIFY – She appears as a thin woman in rags, carrying a bag with the bottom ripped out and a broken cup or phone. I have seen both.

ELEMENTS/MATERIALS OF PREFERENCE – gold, diamonds, watches

DESIRES – seeking clarity

DEFENSIVE ACTIONS, CAUTION – use to create insanity, confusion, or to change the age of yourself or others. Once the Sorcery Event is in motion you must take charge, as SCREW 779 is not very capable in the areas of continuity or completion. She will push back and create confusion if not monitored. She feels to me as if she is a woman who fell out of her life from the sky.

TRIBUTES – I suggest keeping one of her elements available for her to use or have at her disposal so she can focus on it, but I have never seen her pick one up.

DEALS – she has never asked for a deal

EVOCATION – Wrap a broken doll in a small blanket and sing to it as if you are in mourning. As you do this, write her number, 779 frantically on some kind of dated material such as a newspaper. This is how I discovered her. The number came to me and I was writing it repeatedly on the NY Times. I didn't know why but I felt it was important. The broken doll was on the table and we had intended to take it to a restorer to be fixed. She attached to it and mourned it so continuously that I had to bury it with a proper funeral. Once she is in the room, tell your desires to her as if engaging her in a story making sure to tuck into that story the details of that which you desire. During your story, stop and ask her to repeat those sections to you, and that which she repeats will be that which occurs. She doesn't 'go and do your bidding' in the way other Daemons do.

The repeating of your words act like ritual and the results are the fulfillment of your desires. The manner in which she leaves is as tragic as is she herself. She simply walks away sobbing.

AN INTERACTION

If you are of the mindset to handle sadness as a usable energy – then this is the Daemon with whom you should consider working. She is a fragile mess, however – she delivers a clear and powerful result. After working with her you may feel a deep and profound sadness. This is the Static

Practice at the high efficiency end if you can handle the sadness and turn it into energy for Sorcery – fuel yourself with it.

Also..... does the name Dorian Gray bring anything to mind.....?................

TWENTY TWO

PITCHER JOHN

– He is a dangerous boy who sharpens or distorts memories or removes the ability to remember anything at all. He also controls bees, wasps and hornets. He leaves when he is ready to go.

CAUTION – If there are children or persons exceedingly sensitive or susceptible to suggestion, or persons who are differently abled in a way that makes them vulnerable, do not evoke Pitcher John in your home.

PITCHER JOHN

HISTORY/STORY – He has not been clear about his origin, as his deception and need for illusion seems to be a vital part of his personality. He is dangerous to work with and one should not summon him for Sorcery unless one has established a relationship with him. Establish this relationship by offering him his elements many times and asking nothing in return. This prior relationship is necessary as he can turn on the Sorcerer if not handled in this manner. I have a sense that he is from the 1920's Scotland. He is a 20th century Daemon but do not let his 'youth' lull you into a false sense of security. On this list of 26 Daemons he is the one with whom I have the closest relationship. I know him well and know that he is the most dangerous of all.

HOW TO IDENTIFY – He is a small knotty strong boy carrying a clock and a knife. The clock looks like a large pocket watch and the knife is quite primitive. He is often followed by flying insects with stingers.

ELEMENTS/MATERIALS OF PREFERENCE
iron, magnets, clockwork pieces, glass lenses, agitated bees or wasps

DESIRES – to control our memories and our ability to decipher them

DEFENSIVE ACTIONS – use to control or change another's memories and to cause bees, hornets and wasps to swarm or leave

TRIBUTES - Sweet delicacies, parchment, beautiful blank books

DEALS - he will make a deal with you and I suggest you keep to it. He is vengeful if he is not respected. Pitcher John uses bees to enact revenge on Practitioners who do not keep agreements.

EVOCATION– invite him to visit with you often by creating a black box filled with his elements. Paint his name backwards on the box, just as in his sigil. Leave it for him and say Hello John every time you pass by the box. Do this continuously. After a period of time you will notice him hanging around the box, eventually playing with its contents. You may hear the buzzing of stinging insects but they cannot harm you as he has not been disrespected by you. He can however call upon living stinging insects to attack if provoked so remember to keep all agreements and never remove anything from the box. Speak to him calmly as one would speak to a lunatic with a gun. As you eventually gain his trust you can ask him for a favor. If he is going to do your bidding he will act it out in front of your before he does it. Clap for him and tell him how grateful you are. He may or may not leave after his work for you is done. Do not remove the box. If you do bees will begin to follow you. That is how to deal with this Pitcher John.

AN INTERACTION

My life with Pitcher John is private....

TWENTY THREE
FLYD GLUTD -
controls freedom, escape or fleeing, use parole or imprison

HISTORY/STORY – Flyd Glutd developed through the combination of tortured prisoners and those fleeing from natural disasters. This once seemed to be a genderless Daemon. Recent work has shown me that this Daemon is Male. He has become more tangible since the first edition of this book. Flyd Glutd is useful to get prisoners out, shorten the sentence, or enhance the possibility of parole. He is also useful for getting a speedy divorce, encouraging the other person to leave in a situation where you feel trapped or overwhelmed, or helping to vacate a position of employment or partnership, including sexual partnership, which you desire.

How to Identify - He is a tall thin man of neat attire with the look of an old school New York gangster, reverent and elegant.

ELEMENTS/MATERIALS OF PREFERENCE – iron, keys, sound of machines grinding metal

DESIRES – to experience the energy of those who are fleeing, or those who are captured and planning escape

DEFENSIVE ACTIONS – Evoke Flyd Glutd to rid yourself of or detain an individual, or to gain freedom or partnership where another partner must be removed so that you can take that place

TRIBUTES – none

DEALS - For that which you keep you must also set something free. He may ask for your assistance in Sorcery works that do not come from your desires.

EVOCATION – sprinkle iron filings over hot coals, shake keys and ask for his help. If he will help you the coals will spark and flame. If not, they will go out. It is that simple. As he does not desire to be kept or detained in any way, he will leave when done.

AN INTERACTION

Free the ones you desire to free...capture or retain imprisonment for the ones who should be kept away...... This Daemon will either perform or not. No hangover, no residual outcome, yes or no.... and if you get a no try other Daemon or change your request...

TWENTY FOUR
188 – remove or cause stress and tension on individual or group

HISTORY/STORY – I call this Daemon 188 because it told me that 188 (no description of ounces or grams or any other measurement) is how much tension weighs. It may or may be genderless, that is not clear. It sounds masculine but leaves no additional clues. For the sake of simplicity I will refer to this Daemon as male.

HOW TO IDENTIFY - He is a red light which pools at the bottom, as if it is about to run like a pool of red wine.

ELEMENTS/MATERIALS OF PREFERENCE
frayed wire, course rocks, black sand, lava rocks, broken locks that will not open

DESIRES - control tensions between humans

DEFENSIVE ACTIONS – use to cause chaos, stress or tensions for an individual or amongst a group of humans. He does not work on animals.

TRIBUTES – you must work silently when summoning him

DEALS - He has never asked for one.

EVOCATION – This may seem overly simplified, but it is just this. Paint his sigil with red paint or ink upon any of his elements. He presented the sigil in the red light so it comes directly from him. Sit quietly and wait to feel interrupted by a nervous or chaotic feeling disturbing the quiet and a sensation that you are to be interrogated. You will see the red light. Ask him for that which you desire. When you are done, remain still until you are once again calm. There is no other technique or issue. If he agreed to do the work the results will be seen quickly. If not then ask again at a later time, changing at least one variable. Keep the sigil for your altar/workspace to use again when evoking him.

AN INTERACTION

If manipulation is an art form, 188 is the materials needed. Stress plays an important part in the work of understanding the Static Practice. Stay on the center line, use the energy of stress that you are experiencing and 'paint' with it. Send it where it best serves you....it is that simple and that powerful. Not for the faint of heart or for karma surfers.....

TWENTY FIVE
Serp-Hant Ave'

a delicious Daemon of epicureanism,
intentional selfishness, self-appreciation and
a well-developed sense of vanity.
Drawn to those who have put their own
needs before the needs of others

HISTORY/STORY – This androgynous Daemon is the de'Sade of the group, enjoying both genders. Serp-Hant Ave' has an essence of being the envy of all others, a royal presence, an undeniable sense of entitlement.

HOW TO IDENTIFY – Serp-Hant Ave' appears as one may think of Mozart. Slight, strong, giddy, perplexing and mystical all at once.

ELEMENTS/MATERIALS OF PREFERENCE –
silk, beautiful stones and beads in the amber and garnet family, brightly colored lizards, fur

DESIRES – to make delight, beauty and joy prevail

DEFENSIVE ACTIONS – can make these temptations drive a person to obsession and madness

TRIBUTES – shiny wings of beetles left in beautiful glass containers

DEALS – none

EVOCATION – He is best brought forward by talking about him, using his name, during moments of debauchery and pleasures. Intoxication is helpful but not absolutely necessary. Evoking him during orgasm also has its advantages as he will stay longer and is more willing to speak. He will laugh aloud at your request, taunting and mocking in a playful manner. He will question your motivations as an amusement. His mocking and imitation may feel annoying but it is his way. He is the only Daemon on this list who has listened to my desires and suggested that I desire more and more, greater and more excessive outcomes. He does not need an exit ritual as he bores easily and will not be back unless evoked.

AN INTERACTION

I have one suggestion to the Practitioner who chooses to work with Serp-Hant Ave'. First, use him on yourself, seeking his energy to open yourself up to that which pulses inside of you. Seek your 'inner de'Sade" through work with Serp-Hant Ave'. By this I mean that if we are inhibited, we are controlled by those inhibitions. Knowing one's true desires and proclivities and controlling them to our own advantage is what libertarians have that allows them to command their lives in a significant way.

TWENTY SIX
CHAGATATHY

manipulates armies, war and ego,
controls the minds of soldiers and
followers

HISTORY/STORY – An 'associate' of NOHG, who has chosen to go on to a more controlling and cerebral approach

HOW TO IDENTIFY – He appears as a swirl of ash first then a large bear like animal.

ELEMENTS/MATERIALS OF PREFERENCE – none noticed

DESIRES – He wants to be consulted when other Daemons have gone rogue. He has an alpha feel, as if he is a pack leader who sleeps alone.

DEFENSIVE ACTIONS – Chagatathy grabs holds of other Daemons when they are acting in a manner dangerous to the doer

TRIBUTES – none that have been noticed

DEALS – his deals are made with other Daemons

EVOCATION – The evocation is similar to the one used for Nohg. Paint his sigil on a small piece of parchment and on another piece write down your desire and roll it into a scroll around a piece of black metal (iron, steel). For this a hand cut steel nail works well. Concentrate on his sigil. You do not have to wait until you hear or see him. Once you feel you have concentrated enough to see your desire, place the scroll on the sigil and bite into your lip. With Blood in your saliva spit onto the scroll and the sigil.

Unroll the scroll and if he has heard you the metal will feel hot and may even leave a mark on the words you have written on the scroll. If the metal is hot and/or has left a mark on the writing, using a pin, harvest Blood from the top of your hand near the knuckles. This will hurt. He too seeks the suffering. Drip one drop of Blood onto the metal and another one onto the sigil. If you do not do this part of the evocation you may allow for inhabitation or possession. Complete the ritual and use the piece of metal to break something that is glass. Take the broken pieces of glass and throw them into moving water. If you do not complete the ritual you risk inhabitation.

AN INTERACTION

Evoke Chagatathy when you have a desire to manipulate large scale change or group thought. I will leave it at that...

* *

THE GLASS RITUAL

Use this ritual when you are seeking the pure energy of Daemons, and not sure which one to invite to participate in your work.

When working with Daemons it is also possible to force the energy of the work into a more focused format by use of The Glass Ritual. If your work with Daemons is focused on destroying a particular individual who has exhibited a behavior that renders that person in need of serious correction, consider The Glass Ritual.

Obtain the glass container that comes with large pullout candles. Place a small magnet in the glass with the positive polarity facing upward. Fill it half way with unclean stagnant water. Create an effigy of the individual in soap so that it will melt in the process. Make it small enough to fit into the glass. Twist an iron or steel nail into the temple of the effigy until it stays well embedded. On small bits of paper write the name of the individual and other identifiable traits such as a birthmark, his address, a business he may own and things of this nature. Roll each one into a tiny ball and drop them into the water.

Tie the effigy with a ribbon around its feet. Tie the other end to a twig, preferably from the property of the individual. Place the twig across the top of the glass and roll the ribbon up by turning the stick. Set it so that you can now place the effigy head first into the water and lower him in slowly and with great intention to cause him suffering. Take your time. When you have completed this portion of the work, let only his feet stick up out of the stagnant water. Remember that all of these actions create triggers which release energy. The energy released is that which causes the outcome.

Make a small amount of clay from flour and water. Create a vessel that is shaped like a tulip with a small opening at the top. Allow the clay to dry overnight. Place inside the opening your freshly harvested Blood and one of the following: Menstrual Blood (can be a stored and dried bit), semen, female sexual fluids or a combination of these items.

Place additional twigs from his property on top of the glass and balance your clay tulip upon the twigs. This sets you above his head and on his mind at all times while at the same time he feels caged. Surround the glass with any or all of the following with the points facing toward the glass:

Iron or Steel nails
Iron or Steel Scissors opened as if to cut the glass
Broken glass shards

Now that the jar is well set, welcome Daemonic energy to feed on him. In less than 30 days the liquid will shoot out of the glass in a volcanic eruption. Once that happens you know he is in any manner of pain and suffering from this work and that you now have control over his wellness. Bury the remains of the work on his property in a shallow 'grave', and once the glass is under the soil smash it with an iron or steel device or the heel of your boot.

At this point, if you feel there is more to do, evoke any of the Daemons from this group that feel appropriate for a continuance of a specific manner of torture or justice. Proceed as he is now wide open to your Sorcery so the work of any of these Daemons which feel appropriate will get into to him with little to no effort.

Be prepared for him to suffer greatly....

26 (27?)

Daem  ons

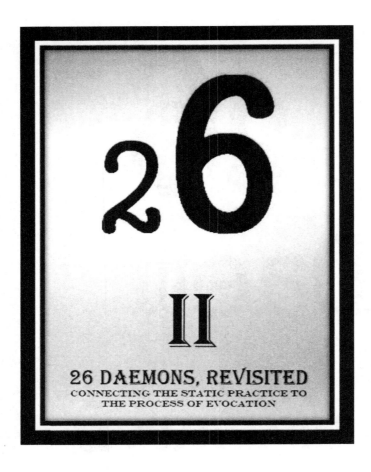

II

26 DAEMONS, REVISITED
CONNECTING THE STATIC PRACTICE TO
THE PROCESS OF EVOCATION

26 Daemons Revisited by
THE SORCERESS CAGLIASTRO
Blood Sorceress, Necromancer in the hands of 9
Copyright 2014

Edited by Pamela Gray, the SWIP at North Sea Tales